POLITICAL COMMUNICATIONS

POLITICAL COMMUNICATIONS

The General Election Campaign of 1979

Edited by
ROBERT M. WORCESTER
MARTIN HARROP

London
GEORGE ALLEN & UNWIN
Boston   Sydney

George Allen & Unwin (Publishers) Ltd,
40 Museum Street, London WC1A 1LU, UK

George Allen & Unwin (Publishers) Ltd,
Park Lane, Hemel Hempstead, Herts HP2 4TE, UK

Allen & Unwin, Inc.,
9 Winchester Terrace, Winchester, Mass. 01890, USA

George Allen & Unwin Australia Pty Ltd,
8 Napier Street, North Sydney, NSW 2060, Australia

First published in 1982

British Library Cataloguing in Publication Data

Political communications: the General Election
    campaign of 1979.
    1. Great Britain. *Parliament* — Elections, 1979-
    I. Worcester, Robert M.   II. Harrop, Martin
    324.941′ 0857   JN956

    ISBN 0-04-324007-0

Library of Congress Cataloging in Publication Data

Main entry under title:
Political communications.
    Based on a conference held at Newcastle upon Tyne
Apr. 1980.
    Includes index.
    1. Elections — Great Britain — Congresses. 2. Great
Britain. Parliament — Elections, 1979 — Congresses.
3. Communication in politics — Great Britain — Congresses.
I. Worcester, Robert M.   II. Harrop, Martin.
JN956.P64   324.941′ 0857   81-22804
ISBN 0-04-324007-0   AACR2

Set in 10 on 11 point Times by Typesetters (Birmingham) Limited,
and printed in Great Britain
by Billing and Sons Limited, Guildford, London and Worcester.

Contents

Introduction

The series of Nuffield election studies began the 'science' of psephology in 1945. 'Psephos', Greek for 'stones', signified the white and black stones which were used as election counters in the Greek city-states' elections over 2,000 years ago. The term was coined by Dr David Butler of Nuffield College, Oxford, a research assistant on the *British General Election of 1945* book and author or co-author of the ten subsequent studies. Yet, despite the proliferation of electoral studies since the war, little attention has so far been paid specifically to political communications. Blumler and others have looked at political broadcasting, Seymore–Ure and others at the political press and Abrams, Leonard, Crewe and Rose at political polling, but scant attention has been given to political communications, to the inter-active dialogue between the elected and the elector, the politician and the demos.

Even in the absence of a comprehensive Nuffield series, the United States has produced a number of studies which have at least scratched the surface of political communication. In particular, the Kennedy Institute's 'Campaign '72: the managers speak' and 'Campaign for President: the managers look at '76', though both somewhat un-structured, did have the virtue of combining and comparing the experiences of politicians, political apparatchik, pollsters, political journalists and academic psephologists. These seminars and the resulting books stimulated the idea of a similar conference here.

The idea for a seminar, and for this book, was to provide a forum for the interchange of ideas and impressions between those academics engaged in the study of communications within the political process and practitioners in the field of political communications, including politicians, press and television, pollsters, and advertising and public relations experts. We wanted, in particular, to provide a forum for the discussion of political communication by those who had taken an active part in a specific political event.

The intention was not only to provide a forum for prepared papers, but to give time for discussion between the participants. To this end, we invited papers from a broad spectrum of people involved in the election. The invited papers not only provided an original contribution to academic knowledge in their own right, but also stimulated a broader discussion between the participants. Many of the papers and the edited version of the discussions that ensued are presented here. The limitations of space dictated by the publisher meant that several excellent contributions to the seminar programme had to be deleted and others shortened considerably.

In structuring the book, we believed that there were four reasonably clear lines of demarcation between the participants in the communications exercise represented by the 1979 general election: there were the advertisers, visible as never before; the politicians 'on the ground'; the media generally and political journalists specifically; and the pollsters and psephologists. This framework provided the structure of the book. At the end of each of the four sections we offer a taste of what proved at the conference to be a very stimulating and useful series of discussions. In this way we hope to have produced a more complete, and complex, picture of the process of political communication, using as a case study the British general election of May 1979.

Like the election itself, the conference brought together a number of professions, whose representatives differed not only in their conception of the election, but also in their criteria of appraisal. Of these professions, it is perhaps only the politicians who judge the election primarily by its outcome – although politicians may 'win' an election even when their party loses and, more rarely, lose when their party wins. The pollsters can assess their performance, and certainly are assessed by others, in terms of the accuracy of their final predictive polls. For the professional communicator, evaluation takes the less precise but still real form of judgements within the advertising profession of which side produced the 'better' (more creative?, more notorious?, more effective?) campaign material. And the broadcasters have their own specialist and arguably conflicting criteria: a desire, on the one hand, to avoid causing undue offence to the politicians, combined with a desire to reform politician–broadcaster relationships such that it matters less whether the politicians *do* take offence. All these criteria, and more, are invoked at various points in this book.

Differing criteria reflect differing expectations. The academic brings to his election a model of rational decision-making where goals are clearly specified and means systematically compared. The communicator from advertising brings expectations based on experience of precise, well-defined relationships between agency and client. And the pollster brings an expectation that the chief problem in responding to public opinion is the technical problem of identifying public opinion. One way of interpreting the material in this book is as a confrontation of these expectations both with each other and with the mundane reality of elections as essentially *political* events in which decisions, to the extent that they are taken at all, are based on an eclectic mixture of ritual, self-interest, intuition, soft fact and softer analysis.

In his concluding remarks at the conference, Bob Worcester posed a number of issues that had been raised, but not fully answered, by the proceedings. These were, somewhat amended and expanded here, as follows:

During (and between) general elections, how much does the public (electorate?) *want* to know?

How much does the public (electorate?) *already* know? And how much of that is incorrect or misconceived?

Does the public understand the *system*, the *issues*, the *choices*?

What segments of the public care or don't care, are informed or are un- or misinformed? And which segments are set in their minds or alternatively (for the parties) can be switched?

Which are the *media* of preference, of audience segmentation, of convenience, of cost, of weight and reach, of value?

What of the *language/semantics* of the electorate? What does the electorate understand us to be saying? Is this appropriate to the audience? What is the impact? The symbolism?

Is *failure* to communicate effectively the fault of the content?, the language?, the medium? – or the 'gate-keepers', the pundits, the commentators? Are these part of the problem or part of the solution?

How should *political parties'* efforts be balanced between the undecided and the party faithful? What will replace demography as the principal determinants of voting as these ties observably weaken?

And what are the *responsibilities* of the politicians, the public, the media and the polls?

The conference served as the inaugural meeting of the Political Communications Study Group of the Political Studies Association, a group which should be able to provide a forum for continuing the work we have begun. We are grateful to the PSA for its support, and to Hugh Berrington, Head of the Department of Politics at the University of Newcastle upon Tyne, for his help in organising and hosting the conference. The conference itself was held at Newcastle in April 1980, long enough after the election for a distillation of reflections, yet not so long as to allow crisp memories to fade.

In preparing the manuscript we appreciated the helpful and efficient work of Terry Donnelly in Newcastle and Marian Rummer in London.

Robert M. Worcester and Martin Harrop
London and Newcastle

Part One

The Advertisers

1

The Politics of Communication, or the Communication of Politics

BARRY DAY

'Electoral communications' has traditionally been one of those multi-syllable and somewhat questionable concepts we British left to the Americans who had – as we all knew – their funny little ways. In any case, they didn't really seem to understand that elections were to do with chaps standing up and telling people what was good for them.

And if those people didn't seem to be getting the point, saying it *louder*.

Of course, they really hadn't been in this election business for five minutes anyway, so what could you *expect*?

If by some strange chance, a group of political 'experts' *had* compared notes after the event, say, in 1959, there might have been a grudging nod to those advertising chappies – what were their names? Colman, Prentis and Varley? – for having come up with a jolly good slogan.

Except that, of course, by the current criteria of those days, if your party had *lost*, it was obviously a very bad slogan and, if they'd *won*, the line of people who'd *really* thought of it would stretch from here to Smith Square . . .

In simple terms, as far as most politicians were concerned, irrespective of party – the possible contribution of advertising, its techniques and its technicians to the electoral process was perceived as being located somewhere between trivialisation and heresy. To many people, it probably still is.

Nevertheless, it's unarguable that over the last two decades, advertising *has* taken a place in the political process. The only argument is *what* place?

I don't think we can properly evaluate the pros and cons of 1979 without taking a brief look at the time context and tracing a few of the media manifestations back to their roots. How did we *get* to where we are?

It's ironic that even as we speak – so to speak – the Republican Party in the USA is studying the Conservative campaign of 1979. Full circle – or full spiral. Ironic because just about everything that's been done in this country of any significance – certainly in the last ten years – can trace its origins back to American precedent.

There's the technique of the Blurred Promise or the Unprovable Assertion. As King Lear put it:

I will do such things – what they are yet I know not – but they shall be the terrors of the world.

It's a classic political posture.

Advertising didn't *invent* it. It just *conveyed* it.

Eisenhower used it in 1956. He did a series of short commercials on topical issues. Each spot would pose a crucial question – to which he would reply something like: 'Mamie worries about the same thing. I tell her it's our job to change that on November . . .' When the filming was finished, he was also heard to lament 'To think that an old soldier should come to this'.

Then there's the technique of What We Are *Not*. The politics of fear. Sometimes it is the fear of the Unknown Alternative. Sometimes the fear of More of the Same. As somebody once said – 'Oppositions don't *win* elections. Governments *lose* them'.

President Johnson, if you remember, won hands down in 1964, not by what he said *he* would do, but by making the American public focus on the unspeakable alternative.

One Democrat commercial showed a small girl picking the petals off a flower while the soundtrack used the countdown to a nuclear blast . . . the reference being to Goldwater's hard-line policy. The result of the campaign – of which this was, admittedly, a small part – was to place Goldwater somewhere to the right of Genghis Khan in the public imagination.

The film itself only ran once, but the public discussion that this little capsulisation generated pinpointed Goldwater's position on that particular issue and put him on the defensive in a way that no conventional utterance could have achieved in anything like the time.

By the mid-1960s – for better or for worse, depending on how you view these things – the techniques of commercial advertising had become an expected (if not necessarily an accepted) part of electoral communications in the USA.

One might have asked: what took them so long?

Advertising, after all, has spent many years and a great deal of various manufacturers' money learning how to compress a lot of information into a little space, keeping a message simple and relevant to as many people as possible – and then giving it immediacy and impact.

All of the things that a politician needs his utterances to achieve.

Americans – being people who hold successful salesmanship in high esteem – were quick to appreciate advertising for what it was. Another tool of the political salesman's trade to be weighed in the public emotional balance like anything else.

I believe – I hope – we're well beyond that rather spurious debate of the late 1960s, when the 'New Politics' were all the rage and there were people who seriously thought that the communicators, the by now Far-From-Hidden Persuaders, had inherited the political earth and that a candidate for a party could be elected, given an intelligent face and a few quotable lines to be declaimed on prime-time television.

Not necessarily so.

Ask Teddy Kennedy. Ask George Bush. Ask a few dozen local and national American politicians who've spent a few million dollars over the last decade to find themselves precisely nowhere.

Visibly and publicly – nowhere.

In the USA, at least, the communication contribution is now safely in perspective. At least, for now. Here, in the UK, I'm not so sure.

To anyone who's studied the subject, the furore over advertising's part in the 1979 election had a touch of *déjà vu*. Only the names had been changed to protect the innocent. Or not so innocent. The whole thing was slightly out of sync, because it wasn't even all that *new*. Except in the amount and to the degree.

The first deliberate attempt to apply some of the relevant lessons of US experience – and therefore, as far as I can determine, the first *conscious* effort to use the established techniques of commercial marketing on the *British* political scene, came in the 1970 election on behalf of the Conservative Party.

The programme was controlled by a tightly knit little group of professional communicators. The group was composed of four key elements that were fundamental to its eventual success and which, I suspect, are key to any comparable operation.

There was the *Political* representative – in that case, Willie Whitelaw (then Chief Whip) – who acted as the 'client' and who could and did say an immediate yes or no with the full authority of the parliamentary party. That speed of decision, that ability to prevent decisions becoming bogged down in those endless committees that spring up, hydra-headed, during elections, was critical.

Then there was the *Party* representative (Sir Michael Fraser) from Conservative Central Office. He could deliver the party 'machine'.

Focus of the group was the *Director of Publicity* (Geoffrey Tucker), temporarily a party employee but essentially a professional secondment from the world of advertising and marketing.

Finally, the *specialists* from the fields of advertising and film making.

A cohesive, unified team with clear terms of reference.

It was up to the party to decide on policy and content – it was up to the specialists to communicate it as effectively as possible with all the techniques at our disposal.

In terms of media, we were limited.

A certain amount of national and regional press advertising – mostly handled by the advertising agency, whose contribution was limited to that. No posters. At that time, they were considered to contravene electoral law *during* an election campaign. No paid television – unlike the USA.

What we *did* have – and the example I'd like to use briefly to illustrate the points – were the Party Political Broadcasts, something quite unique in Western society, as far as I'm aware. I think the temporary advantage we had at that time was the utter disregard into which the PPBs had sunk. There you were with fifty minutes of prime-time TV, with nothing else for the viewer to watch while you were on – something which would cost you hundreds of thousands of pounds commercially, *if* you could buy it.

And the parties were getting it *free*. Perhaps that's why they didn't appreciate it. With very rare exceptions, in the past the parties had reduced the PPBs to the viewing level of a Boris Karloff B-picture – *The Curse of the Talking Head.*

Our perception was rather different.

We felt we shouldn't regard the time as five ten-minute slots, but as fifty *cumulative* minutes of the Tory Story, so to speak. The communication should build as the campaign built . . . and we wrote up another maxim that still seems to me to be basic: *Be prepared to adapt*. Whatever an election campaign *seems* to be about when it starts, it tends to be about other things as it evolves.

Too rigid planning can end up in irrelevant communication.

We felt that to get through with our message we must apply the obvious lessons of the editorial media.

In this TV age, people expect to get their news information and certainly the commentary on that information from the media. Particularly TV.

Panorama, News at Ten – programmes like those were the touchstone of opinion for the people we had to reach. Just as they had been in the States for many years. Their anchormen were judge and jury in the pubs and clubs. If Old Robin (Day) gave a particular politician a going-over on the box, well, you'd never rated him anyway, had you?

So why not have our *own* programme? In that way we could blend with the media background.

Our anchormen could be two well-known faces. Both of them *happened* to be Tory politicians but their previous connection with *editorial* TV was where they had established that familiarity in the first place.

The Chris Chataway/Geoffrey Johnson–Smith Show was called *A Better Tomorrow*, and if they were perhaps a little more partisan than Robin Day or Reginald Bosanquet would have been, that, after all, was political show business and their commentary was 'objective' within the political definition of that word.

Having created the 'editorial' context of the programme format, we still felt the need for the capsulisation the TV commercial can uniquely provide.

And again, facing the facts of this day and age, if you want to cut through the information clutter the people out there are subjected to and get a simple point home to them, it was (and is) a fact of modern life that the TV commercial is now one of the key ways in which people *expect* to get their information. It's the way that choices are posed.

We couldn't *buy* commercials, but there was nothing that said we couldn't put them into our own programmes – the party political broadcasts.

The essence of a TV commercial is its single-minded simplicity. One commercial showed a £1 note – shades of Wilson's 'pound in the pocket' – being brutally attacked by a pair of scissors. As each segment was snipped away, a voice-over stated the date and depleted value of the pound, ending with the inescapable fact that the continuation of Labour policies would lead to the 'ten-bob pound'.

Another showed a woman's hand taking a block of ice from a domestic fridge. Embedded in the ice was a frozen wage packet. Labour gave it to you last time. Vote for them, 'and you'll get it again – in the family economy size'.

The sharpness of the commercial can be used to probe. Wilson was the master of the sweeping assertion when it suited him but equally prone to emulate the closeness of the clam when it didn't. One commercial used the soundtrack to voice the legitimate questions of the electorate: 'What about Wedgwood Benn?' 'Are you going to pay the doctors?' 'What about all these strikes?' Meanwhile the camera moved inexorably in on the face of Harold Wilson. 'This is the deafening silence of Mr Wilson. Why is it that a man who's so good at *asking* questions is so bad at *answering* them?'

And towards the end of the campaign we added a final commercial after the programme 'credits' in which a hand hovered over a voting slip which offered two choices – 'More of the same' or 'A better tomorrow'. The voice-over posed the decision facing the voter: 'How you vote is your business. It doesn't cost you anything and it doesn't take a moment. But with the wrong decision – you could have quite a price to pay.' Down came the pen in the 'right' square.

We felt that this capsulisation, this attempt to simplify some complexities, was a vital element in our communications plan – particularly as the days dwindled down to a precious few.

What was the election really all *about*? Whatever Harold Wilson *hoped* it was about, it became clear that the cost of living was what concerned people most. The diminishing pound in their pockets. Wage inflation was going unchecked, so money was pouring into the male wage packet, but for some strange reason, Mr Wilson happened to have called an election before the full result of that inflation could be felt in the housewife's shopping basket.

We had to get that thought into her mind and yet few electorates are good at anticipating things to come, especially if they're bad news. We wanted to sum up what we thought the election was about in a simple phrase that could be used in speeches, quoted by the media and generally stick in the public mind. We called it – *The Shopping Basket Election.*

It seemed to serve that purpose. The media picked it up as a handy gap. Several newspapers – until the newspaper strike – used a shopping basket graphic on a regular basis to check the cost of living as the days went by.

We did one other thing that broke a certain amount of new ground in applying proved marketing practice to political theory. Within our general electorate we defined a specific target segment for special media attention – and we did it by changing direction and emphasis while the campaign was under way. In fact, within the last week or so.

By this time, the Conservative Party had been doomed to defeat by the opinion polls. The only ray of light was that repressed majority, the working-class housewife.

She'd never had it so bad.

Even wives of traditional Labour supporters were getting edgy. Was there a chance that for the first time we could disturb the historical class voting pattern of the working-class family and persuade *her* to vote differently from her husband?

True, women were sensing their own separate identity more and more, but were *these* women ready for *this*?

We found Sylvia, a typical example of this new social phenomenon and let her put our case for us. Without any prompting, Sylvia found the words for us from her own experience. Here was a working woman in her early twenties, married with one child. They had a car, 'and I think that's about all we will have'.

Their joint earnings went every week with no chance to save anything ('And it's not as if I squander – because I haven't anything to squander.') If her husband got a wage increase, it was immediately taken up in tax. There was 'no incentive for people like us'.

So far, a problem common to the electorate as a whole but the knife went in when Sylvia declared that, although her husband would probably vote Labour again because of his family voting tradition ('He's not easily persuaded'), she most certainly would not.

Labour, she felt, didn't understand a woman's problems. The Conservatives must make the country better, 'because they can't make it any worse'. She felt it was time to give them a chance.

Ironically, the strongest motivation for electoral reversal is as simple as that – time for a change.

For what it's worth, subsequent research showed that a substantial number of working-class women *did* vote Conservative for the first time. But that really isn't the point. It was the defining of a new target market under pressure and the focusing of communication effort against it that was significant. Plus the flexibility and control to implement the decision immediately, once it was made.

1970 was a very good year for the Tories. There was a team that worked decisively and well. There was trust in the air. There was a determination to do things differently. There was machinery to turn decision into action.

The 1980s was to be our decade. We would, of course, need two terms to do it all. But now that we'd got the hang of communicating, government was going to be very different. No more civil service bureaucracy. Open government from now on. But that was then.

By 1974 that same party, now in power and dignified by the name 'government', had forgotten many of the lessons we had all learned the hard way.

And perhaps this remains the most significant lesson of all.

It's all too easy for the party that *wins* an election to feel itself 'sanctified' by winning and becoming government.

Too easy to forget what got it there and to lose some of its *political* edge, to allow itself to be shut off from certain realities that it understood perfectly well on the way to winning. What a party does in government is also legitimately *party* political ammunition too when an election comes around.

If any conventional advertiser *stopped* advertising when he had a brand leader on the market, his competitors would think he was mad. And they would have a point.

Advertising does not work properly on an *ad hoc* basis. Anyone who thinks it does is really saying they don't believe in advertising.

The Tory Party forgot a lot of things by 1974 that it had learned in

1970. It stopped putting its case. It would be quite a few years before it remembered them – and learned a few new ones.

Note: Chapter 1

Barry Day is Vice-Chairman of McCann–Ericson Advertising and served as adviser to the Conservative Party and speech-writer to former Prime Minister Edward Heath between 1969 and 1975.

2

The Conservatives' Advertising Campaign

TIM BELL

In reviewing the work of our agency, Saatchi & Saatchi, for the Conservative Party in the election campaign, it is important to consider the whole period from the spring of 1978. It's then that the strategy was set, a strategy from which we never deviated until the election campaign itself. This, I think, is one of the reasons why if we had any effect at all it was ‑ positive rather than a negative effect. I must also add that my comments refer specifically to the advertising effort, and not necessarily to the Conservative Party's overall strategy.

The Background

Let me begin by reviewing the organisational setting. The controlling group consisted of Lord Thorneycroft, who as Chairman of the Party retained total decision-making power; Gordon Reece, the party's Director of Public Relations, who provided the direct link with the advertising agency which was represented by myself; Alistair McAlpine, the party Treasurer, who was present at most meetings to ensure that the campaign was capable of being paid for; and Chris Patten, Research Director, who checked back that we were continuing to sell policies which fairly represented the party rather than just those we felt were most attractive. Plus the occasional visit from Mrs Thatcher, who would give an over-riding view.

The relationship between the party and the agency was such that we in the agency were able to see virtually any relevant piece of information we wanted concerning party policy or party research. I think Tim Delaney (Labour Party advertising adviser) would agree that this is one of the key differences between his operation and mine. And there's absolutely no doubt that if you do engage in mushroom management, you will produce inferior results.

Our work can be divided into three phases. The first went up to

Callaghan's decision not to call an election in October 1978. Just to dispel any doubts, we did anticipate an autumn election and so, I suspect, did many people on the other side. This is a very important point in strategic terms, because it meant we were much better prepared for an election in October than the Labour Party. Since we had been doing the promotion and communications work, we had the machine up and working. Although we were all savagely depressed by the then Prime Minister's decision not to call an election, we got ourselves up off the floor within forty-eight hours and were back ready for whenever the fight would take place.

The second phase was the winter of 1979–80, the 'winter of discontent'. This was again a critical period, since it gave us the opportunity to heighten public dissatisfaction with the government, an opportunity which might not have arisen but for the industrial unrest in the country at the time. Although it's an over-simplification to say that 'governments lose elections, oppositions don't win them', it is true that an opposition must use communication techniques effectively to sharpen public dissatisfaction with the government rather than satisfaction with the opposition. Everything we did was directed towards increasing the salience of this dissatisfaction; towards transforming a vague dislike of the circumstances in which people were living into a burning issue for them. We did, of course, propose as well as oppose but it is patently obvious from our work that we spent more time opposing than we did proposing. In short, oppositions win elections by ensuring that governments lose – and that is the opportunity with which we were presented by the winter of discontent. The third phase of our campaign, to which I'll return, was the election campaign itself.

Advertising men write things in one line if they can, because that is all they can possibly work to. I make no apologies at all for saying that advertising, as a form of *mass* communication, is inevitably a blunt, crude, direct instrument. It is not, nor should it be, our business to produce subtlety of detail and explanation. So the message of our work was expressed in terms sufficiently broad and general to allow us to create a personality for what we were saying. And this, very simply, was that a Conservative vote is a vote for freedom, choice, opportunity, small government and prosperity. The notion was that if you asked people what a vote for the Tories means, they should snap out with an answer which in some ways reflects these associations. We were not talking about incomes policies, or tax cuts, or industrial relations legislation, or public expenditure. We were talking about the emotional meaning of a Conservative vote.

This emphasis meant that the tone of voice adopted in the advertising was probably its single most important feature. We wanted a tone which was warm, confident, non-divisive – and exciting. Simple adjectives, admittedly, but adjectives which provided specific objectives for our work. 'Warmth' just means talking with people rather than to or at them. The Conservative Party has long been perceived as a cold and unsympathetic party. This needed to be changed. 'Confidence', on the other hand, was an attribute we worked to *re-create*. Looking at the research over the previous twenty years, we found that the Conservative Party had lost its position as the party ranked by the electorate as the most competent and confident. It was, therefore, essential for us to talk in a confident tone as though we knew that Conservative policies would work.

'Non-divisive' because a national appeal does actually reach further and deeper than a party appeal. The 'one-nation' concept is much more powerful than appealing to any particular position on an ideological spectrum, whether it's the left, the left-middle, the right-middle, or the right. 'Exciting' because we felt that politics had become unbelievably tedious and boring. Here after all was an election which could result in Britain's first woman Prime Minister. That was rather an exciting thought for the general public and we thought it would not hurt to make the whole approach exciting.

The importance of tone to our advertising affected our research strategy. We emphasised qualitative rather than quantitative research. Inside the agency we conducted a number of group discussions designed to identify the emotional attitudes which emerge when ordinary people discuss politics. We filmed nearly all these discussions, so that we could read the faces as well as the words. The importance of these discussions is that they simulate what happens in society. People talk to each other out there and what they say is the biggest influence there is on how they behave. Word of mouth influence is far greater than TV, far greater than radio, far greater than advertising and far greater than the politicians. The bloke who lives next door to you or who stands next to you in the pub has far more influence than anyone else in determining how you vote.

Quantitative research formed a less central part of our research effort. None the less, we did use polling information for two specific, limited purposes. First, to establish what the key issues were in the minds of the voters. These, it turned out, were prices, taxes, wages, the unions and Europe – though Europe had all but disappeared off the bottom of the list by the time of the election campaign itself.

The second purpose was to identify our target market. The target market proved to be very clear and was of great importance in providing a discipline to the campaign. It provided us with a directional signal which influenced our casting, language and media purchases. For this reason, it is worth while describing the target market in detail.

First-time voters were an important part of the target market. There were many people coming into the market for the first time, people who were available to us because of the increase in electoral volatility. It had become clear from all the research work we had seen that the habit of voting the way your father or even your grandfather had voted was no longer as prevalent as it had once been.

Women were an important group for a more obvious reason. With a female leader, we felt women should form part of the target market. A sub-group here in which we took particular interest were the wives of trade union members. All the evidence suggested that these women were fed up to the back teeth with the way the trade unions were behaving. In particular, the way their husbands were behaving, or being forced to behave by the unions, was obviously causing great resentment. We felt that the idea of a woman being able to run things better than a man would have a natural appeal for the wives of union members.

Skilled workers had suffered an erosion of traditional pay differentials between themselves and unskilled workers. Whatever the causes of this erosion, our research suggested that the tax-cutting issue was a powerful one for this group. Skilled workers, then, also formed part of the target market.

And, finally, *the faithful*. You can never forget your own supporters even though there was nowhere else for ours to go. We never for one moment imagined there would be a Liberal resurgence, an assumption which turned out to be reasonably accurate.

The distribution of advertising between the various media was designed to reach the target market I have described. We concentrated our *newspaper* advertising on the tabloids: the *Express*, the *Mail*, the *Mirror* and the *Sun* from the dailies, and the *Sunday Mirror*, the *Sunday People* and the *News of the World* from the Sundays. Our *magazine* use concentrated on women's magazines in order to reach the female audience. Here, however, we faced a difficulty in that we were unable to use IPC publications, which refused to carry political advertising. To reach the young, first-time voters, we made extensive use of the *cinema*, the first time this medium had been widely used in political advertising. This again led to difficulties. Rank refused to let us use their cinemas throughout, since they did not wish to be associated with a political party. EMI came under pressure from their managers in the election campaign and withdrew our right to use their cinemas. Although this left us with just the independents, the cinema campaign had by then generated publicity of a value far beyond its original cost. We used in addition *posters* and, of course, *party political broadcasts* (PPBs) on radio and television.

Before I discuss examples of our work in each of these media, I would like to comment on the length of PPBs on television. We put in a strong plea for two-minute PPBs, quite prepared to accept a smaller total of television time in order to reduce the length of each PPB. Ten minutes is really the most ludicrous length of time; it is a nightmare for a professional to have to produce to this length. Ten minutes on the same subject is bound to be boring. There are very few television programmes where the same subject will be discussed for more than three or four minutes. It will be interesting in this respect to see whether the five-minute PPBs we introduced in 1980 prove to be more compelling.

THE RUN-UP

Our first television PPB came during a period when Labour had taken the lead in the polls for the first time since April 1976.[1] Before the broadcast, we attempted something that had never been done before. We ran a 'teaser' in the tabloids saying that if you miss television at 9 o'clock tonight you could regret it for the rest of your life. Since no election was imminent at that point, we needed a device to draw people's attention to what we were doing. Incidentally, the law requires the name of the advertiser to appear in the advertisement; the tease would have been far more effective without identification. But the law in its wisdom has decided to protect you.

> This country was once the finest nation on earth. We were famous for our love of freedom, justice and fair play. Our inventions brought the world out of the Middle-Ages to industrial prosperity.
> Today, we are famous for discouraging people from getting to the top. Famous for not rewarding skill, talent and effort.
> In a word, Britain is going backward.

The central section identified the creation of wealth and the redistribution of wealth as the central philosophical difference between the parties, and used plain, simple language to express the implications of these differences for policies on earnings, jobs, prices and productivity. Michael Heseltine summed up as follows: 'Backwards or forwards because we can't go on as we are . . . Don't just hope for a better life – vote for one.'

The final copy-line is worth discussing. The art of slogan-construction is just about the most frightening aspect of working as an advertising man for a political party. All parties say to you: 'Can we have a slogan by tomorrow?' But the point is that we actually don't like the hasty construction of copy-lines. In the commercial world we normally spend several months creating a copy-line and then several years developing an association between copy-line and brand. These opportunities just don't exist in political advertising. Our solution to these problems was to invent a multiplicity of copy-lines and then use them all in different circumstances. We therefore avoided a situation where everyone either liked or disliked one specific copy-line. The PPB and the associated poster campaign caused great controversy. Writing in 1959 about the Conservative advertising produced by Colman, Prentis & Varley, David Windlesham suggested that 'the angry reactions [the advertising] provoked in the Labour Party may have encouraged more people to look at them'.[2] It is interesting to observe exactly the same phenomenon almost twenty years on. The Labour Party reacted strongly to our work and greatly increased their expenditure on advertising in this period. Subsequently, however, the party did learn its lesson and ceased to react to our work.

Figure 2.1

The poster which caused most controversy was, of course, 'Labour isn't working'. Ironically, I had the most awful battle getting the party's approval for this poster. The objection was that since few people would actually read the copy beneath the title, the effect of including the name of the Labour Party in the title would be counter-productive. Yet whatever the veracity of this argument, the poster will probably go down in history as one of the most effective political posters ever produced. (For the record: the dole queue was composed of Young Conservatives from South Hendon and not employees of Saatchi & Saatchi.)

Following the first PPB and the poster campaign, we moved into the women's magazines. Our approach here drew on some classic political advertising from around the world. One advertisement, based on some Australian work, but also previously used in Britain, employed

DO THIS QUIZ TO FIND OUT IF YOU'RE LABOUR OR CONSERVATIVE

Should the choice of your child's school depend on:
a. Whoever happens to be Minister of Education at the time.
b. The amount of money you've got in the bank.
c. Your personal preference based on your child's needs and ability.

If your husband works harder and makes more money should he:
a. Lose most of it in tax.
b. Pay no extra tax at all.
c. Pay a little more tax.

Do you think that owning your own home is:
a. Anti-social.
b. Only for the rich.
c. Something to be encouraged by the government.

Do you think the money from North Sea Oil should be spent on:
a. Nationalising more industries.
b. Bigger social security payments.
c. Cutting taxation, and encouraging industry.

Do you think that old-age pensioners should be:
a. Taxed like everyone else.
b. Taxed more.
c. Taxed less.

Do people leave Britain to work abroad:
a. Because the weather's better.
b. They're unpatriotic.
c. Other countries reward effort more and tax people less.

If you decide on private medical treatment should you be:
a. Discouraged from doing so.
b. Prevented from doing so.
c. Allowed to spend your money as you see fit.

Do you feel that lower taxes and less government spending:
a. Causes inflation.
b. Increases inflation.
c. Helps lower inflation.

In doing a difficult job at a time when crime is increasing and there is a shortage of policemen should the police:
a. Be less well-off than other workers.
b. Be held to the national guidelines on wage increases.
c. Be given special treatment.

Which of these people is more likely to know what it's like to do the family shopping?
a. James Callaghan.
b. Your husband.
c. Mrs. Thatcher.

How did you do?
There are no 'right' or 'wrong' answers.
It all depends what you believe in. But if you answered 'c' to at least one of the questions, you agree with the Conservatives on something.
If you answered 'c' more than once it may or may not surprise you to learn that you agree with many of the aims and beliefs of the Conservatives. If you answered 'c' throughout then it doesn't surprise us that you are one of the millions of women in Britain who knows what's best for the country.

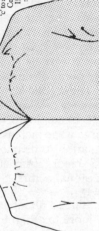

Figure 2.2

the reversed supermarket poster: 'One pinta for the price of two!'; 'Special offer: up eight pence!'; 'Cheddar cheese doubled in price!' Since women's magazines are full of quizzes, we also did a quiz. You'll be surprised to learn that every time you put a tick in box C, you turned out to be a Conservative – and it was impossible not to tick box C. For example:

Should the choice of your child's school depend on:

(a)   Whoever happens to be Minister of Education at the time.
(b)   The amount of money you've got in the bank.
(c)   Your personal preference based on your child's needs and abilities.

This is called a non-divisive appeal.

We then ran an advertisement on law and order, reporting the increase in crime: 'Mugging up 204%', and so forth. Many critics claimed exactly the same thing had happened under the last Conservative government. I must confess I didn't myself see how this negated the point of our advertisement.

The second PPB employed three themes which we used constantly in our work, right through to the election campaign itself. These were tax, unemployment and the economic circle linking high taxation to large wage increases, large wage increases to price inflation, and price inflation to demands for another round of large wage increases. For the record, the circle was demonstrated in the broadcast by professional actors:

> 'Since Labour came to power in 1974 the working man is paying more tax than ever before . . . It would stretch over three hundred miles: Glasgow.'[3]

In the summer of 1979 we launched a cinema commercial aimed at first-time voters. The cinema is an entertainment medium and we set out with this advertisement to entertain an audience. We adopted a deliberately flip tone, more so indeed than in any other political advertisement I have seen from anywhere in the world. I felt personally that it was a wonderfully effective film, in that people either threw ice-cream cornets at the screen or stood in the stalls yelling and cheering. The greatest thing for an advertiser is to get a reaction. If people sit in silence, you might just as well go away and die. We wanted to convey excitement in our campaign and this commercial certainly generated an excited response:

> 'Is this the queue for the 50p stalls? . . . Coming shortly: The Conservatives. A great programme for all the family.'

MUGGING UP 204%*
CRIMINAL DAMAGE UP 135%+
ROBBERY UP 88%+

Labour's record on crime is criminal. Crime is one of the few things in Britain that is booming under Labour.

In England and Wales last year, over 800,000 more crimes were recorded than in 1973.

That's a rise of almost 50%. And yet since Labour came to power, police strength has risen by a mere 7%.

Perhaps if Labour had been more concerned with creating wealth rather than re-distributing it, they might have found it easier to be able to afford to increase policemen's pay. But it's not just more pay our policemen need.

The Government have a duty to be seen to support law and order, to protect people and property.

It certainly doesn't make the police's job any easier when some Labour Ministers are seen associating themselves with scenes of violent extremism, as they did at Grunwick last year.

The police are doing a difficult job, in difficult times–and they need the support of all the people–and that includes Government Ministers.

Without that support, many police-men feel there's only one way they can make the Government understand their plight.

And that's by leaving the force.

IS IT SAFE TO VOTE FOR ANOTHER LABOUR GOVERNMENT?

VOTE CONSERVATIVE [X]

*Figure for London between 1973-1977. †Home Office Annual Criminal Statistics for England and Wales between 1973-1977.
Conservative Central Office, 32 Smith Square, London, S.W.1.

Figure 2.3

WHY EVERY TRADE UNIONIST SHOULD CONSIDER VOTING CONSERVATIVE.

The Labour Party likes to see itself as the party of the working man.

That's how Labour has established such close links with the Trade Unions.

And there's no doubt that there was a time when the Labour Party made real efforts to improve conditions for workers in this country.

But what good have these close ties done the average working man in recent years?

WHAT LABOUR HAS DONE FOR THE WORKING MAN SINCE THE WAR.

Since 1945, both parties have had roughly the same number of years in power.

In over 16 years of Labour government take home pay of the average industrial worker has gone up, in real terms, by 6%.

In the same period of Conservative government take home pay of the average industrial worker has been 10 times better off with the Conservatives.

HAVE THE CONSERVATIVES JUST BEEN LUCKY?

How have the Conservatives managed to do so much more for the working man?

The fact is you can't increase real wages without increasing production.

And Labour haven't managed to get production moving.

Since the war, in the 16 years under Labour, production only went up *half as much* as it did with the Conservative governments. That's why real wages under Labour haven't grown as fast.

Low production means low wages.

High production means high wages.

Frankly, Labour just don't seem to understand how to get production moving. They don't know how to motivate firms to take on more people.

They don't know how to create a climate in which firms can afford to pay people more and produce more.

The key to higher production isn't government hand-outs and subsidies. It's greater incentives to companies and people.

THE LAST 4 YEARS SEEM TO PROVE THE POINT.

In the last few years, the living standards of workers in this country have been badly hit. The Labour government's explanation for this is that Britain has been suffering because the whole world has been suffering.

Well, the fact is that the world did have a bit of a cold – but it seems to be getting over the worst of it. In Britain that cold seems to have turned into double pneumonia.

Look at France. Between 1974-1977 the average French worker saw his real wages, in terms of what they'll buy, go up by over 18%.

In Germany, the average worker saw his real wages go up by 12%.

The average Dutch worker saw his real wages go up by over 11%.

Meanwhile, in Britain, the average industrial worker saw his real wages, in terms of what they will buy, actually go down.

And it isn't just the French, Germans and Dutch who have done better. The British worker has also done worse than, for example, workers in Thailand, S. Korea, Spain, Portugal, Greece, etc.

WHY HAVE BRITAIN'S WORKERS SUFFERED SO BADLY?

In the last four years in Britain, manufacturing production has actually *fallen*. So real wages couldn't grow. Without any growth in production, Labour have had to have one round of wage control after another ...first £6, then £4, then 10%, now down to 5%.

Now if you produce less, you're restricted on what you can earn, and therefore you're also restricted on what you can buy. If you have to buy less, someone else will have to make less, and that's why today there are so many members of British trade unions not making anything. They're out of work.

The tragic truth is that since Labour came to power, another person has joined the unemployment queue every 3 minutes.

This Labour government, the party whose advertising slogan was "Back to work with Labour" has presided over unemployment levels unseen in this country for decades.

Now the amazing thing is this.

Every Labour government since the war has left more people unemployed when it left office than when it came into office.

WHAT'S LABOUR'S PROBLEM?

It is not that Labour don't want to get production and wages rising. Of course they do. It's not that they don't care about the unemployed. Labour's real problem is their basic philosophy.

They still seem to be fighting the class war that Karl Marx saw in the last century.

The Labour Party is still clinging on to the idea of redistributing wealth.

But what is the use of redistributing wealth when the country has very little wealth to redistribute?

For example, if no one was allowed to keep more than £10,000 of their earnings after tax, the rest of us wouldn't even get enough to buy a box of paper tissues every week.

In fact, their idealistic philosophy actually makes things worse. This philosophy makes the people who want to get the best for themselves and their family feel guilty – and the rest envious if they succeed.

The Labour philosophy taxes ambition, enthusiasm, achievement, the very things that create wealth. That's why, as the facts on record show, Labour's aim of redistributing wealth ends up as distributing poverty.

THE TRADE UNIONS & SOCIAL SERVICES.

The Trade Union movement has often fought for better standards of social services, better schools, housing, hospitals, care for the elderly and underprivileged.

The Labour Party has always expressed to the Trade Unions that it has the best intentions in these areas. Sadly, as the past four years have shown, you can't pay for better social services with good intentions. Caring that works costs cash.

It all seems to come down to one thing. Money – and the policies which create it. Labour never seem to have enough. That's strange, you might think, when we're paying more tax under this present Labour government than ever before.

But despite all this tax they're collecting, they still haven't got enough to pay for the proper standards of social services. And they never can get enough coming in from tax, when people aren't earning and producing enough in the first place.

We all know with Labour's production record, people can't earn enough. So the Labour government has to take more and more of what they do earn to

try and pay for the schools, hospitals and social services we all want.

This is not opinion. It is the official government record:

Since the war every Labour government has increased income tax.

And every Conservative government has cut income tax.

Yet every Conservative government since the war has been able to increase the amount spent on social services.

How is this possible? As we've seen since the war, with the Conservatives real earnings rose by ten times more than under Labour.

So Conservative governments could afford to take a smaller share of your earnings in tax and still be left with enough in the kitty to pay for the proper standards of social services we all want.

SHOULD YOU BE VOTING CONSERVATIVE?

The one sure barometer of Labour's support amongst Trade Unionists is the level of financial support industrial members are prepared to give the Labour Party:

a Three quarters of the members of SOGAT now refuse to pay the political levy to the Labour Party.

b Half the membership of TASS have opted out of the Labour levy.

c Two thirds of the members of ASTMS have chosen not to pay the levy.

d One in three members of the National Union of Mineworkers (including many members now retired who spent their whole working lives down the pits) refuse to pay the Labour levy.

In fact, it is reckoned that up to one out of every three Trade Unionist voters now vote Conservative.

Even so, some Trade Unionists may still feel traditionally tied to the Labour Party, and might find it strange to vote Conservative.

To them the Conservative Party makes this promise.

The next Conservative government will concentrate all its efforts to break out of this depressing cycle of low production and low wages – and restore the system of responsible and realistic pay bargaining, free from government interference.

Freedom from government interference has always been a traditional principle of the Trade Union movement – and freedom from government interference is also a traditional principle of the Conservative Party.

Even if you're a lifetime Labour voter, please vote in the coming election on the *actual record* of the two parties.

Because that record seems to prove conclusively that the Conservatives, in trying to look after the nation as a whole, do a better job of looking after the working man than the so-called working man's party.

THE CONSERVATIVE PARTY

The purpose of the third PPB was to show how the economic policies of the Conservative Party related to the theme of care and compassion. We demonstrated that no matter how caring a person you are, if you haven't got the cash you can't afford to care. And if you have, you can. We included William Whitelaw in this broadcast, since he was a good person to speak on care and compassion:

'Who cares about Jane? . . . For our children, because they are our future.'

We then went into the second and in many ways crucial phase of the pre-campaign period: the winter of 1979–80. With the government locked in battle with the unions, we had a strategic opportunity to pick up some trade union votes – and we went tooth and nail for their support. We wrote a double-page spread for all the popular daily newspapers explaining why a trade unionist should vote Conservative. Although that particular advertisement has since won numerous awards for its copy, it was never expected to be read by everybody. Its function was simply to point out that a great deal *can* be said in justification of Conservative trade unionists. That's sometimes how advertising works; that's how that advertisement worked.

Trade Unionists. Confront your television at 9-00pm. tonight.

Conservative Central Office, 32 Smith Square, London, S.W.1.

Figure 2.5

Our next PPB on television drove home the same lesson. The theme of the broadcast was the adverse effect on productivity of the unions' attitudes towards wages and strikes. We again ran a teaser advertisement saying: 'Trade unionists: confront your television at 9 o'clock tonight.' We faced up squarely to the issue involved, ignoring the advice that we must at all costs not mention the word 'confrontation'.

Instead, we turned the issue to our advantage. We used Lord Thorneycroft in the broadcast, a man whose voice of authority and obvious experience makes him ideal for giving a lesson on the real truths of life:

'Labour's policy of low rewards and high taxation, . . . No wonder we're paid less. We produce less.'

As the winter proceeded, our reading of the situation was that the electorate was becoming increasingly tired with a minority government that was simply hanging on to power on a day-by-day, debate-by-debate basis. We therefore ran a poster which said, 'Cheer up! Labour can't hang on for ever'. I regard this as a classic example of good communication. It expresses a very serious message in a simple, amusing and involving way.

CHEER UP!
LABOUR CAN'T HANG ON FOR EVER.

BRITAIN'S BETTER OFF WITH THE CONSERVATIVES.

Published by the Conservative Central Office, 32 Smith Square, Westminster, London SW1P 3HH

Figure 2.6

There followed a complete change of style. With a deteriorating industrial relations situation in the country, Margaret Thatcher did a broadcast on 17 January in which she talked head to camera for nine minutes forty seconds about the industrial problems. We did not write the script for this broadcast, though we did produce it and give advice on how the material could be most effectively presented. Although I'm not a political scientist, my feeling is that this broadcast won her the election. The Labour government had been caught in a position where it had to pretend that nothing was going wrong at all, even though people's homes were surrounded by overflowing dustbins. The Conservatives could therefore present themselves as the party of the nation, as the party which could deal with the problem about which most people in the country were worrying:

'Yes. Technically, this is a party political broadcast . . . We have to learn again to be one nation or one day we shall be no nation.'

The next PPB was an edited version of one of the greatest and certainly the most inspiring speeches from a political platform I have ever seen. This was Harold Macmillan's superlative speech to the Young Conservatives' Annual Conference in February 1979. It perfectly captured the mood of 'Here's a national problem. For God's sake, someone find a solution'. Wherever I have shown this speech, politicians have invariably said that they wished they had an elder statesman of this calibre. It is perhaps a pity for the Labour Party that they were unable to use their elder statesmen in a similar fashion. But whatever your party, whatever your politics, it is surely impossible not to respond to such a marvellous speech:

'The following extracts are from a talk given by Harold Macmillan to . . . We old people can only sit back and pray God's blessing on your labours.'

THE CAMPAIGN

The election campaign was made up of a number of key elements: the manifesto and the speeches that surrounded it; the publicity, including the media events such as the press conferences; and the advertising campaign itself, which is all that I intend to review here. Before I do so, however, I would like to make these preliminary points.

First, our role in the campaign was not confined to party election broadcasts (PEBs). We also produced all the collateral material such as the leaflets that were pushed through your door. This was the first time an agency had produced this material. It's an important point, because it allowed us to present a unified campaign in terms of both content and format. The total effect of the campaign was, therefore, more than the sum of its parts.

Secondly, with the exception of the final television broadcast, all the PEBs were made before the campaign began. In fact, we still have three in the can that were never used at all. This advance preparation enabled us to keep back the famous 'Crisis, what crisis?' broadcast, for example, until the second PEB, even though the Labour Party was I think expecting us to develop this theme right at the start of the campaign.

Thirdly, I'm not sure that any of our television PEBs which were shown in the campaign were as good as our earlier work. I'm convinced that the television work we did in the build-up was twice as effective as our work in the campaign itself.

Our strategy for the campaign work was simple. We were there to point out government failings and that is what we set out to do. We began by picking up Mr Callaghan's statement that the electorate would judge him on his record. We used a 1,400-site national poster campaign coupled with press advertising to say: 'Labour want you to judge them on their record – record inflation, record taxation, record unemployment and record hospital queues.' The hospital issue was helped enormously by NUPE's kind decision to close some hospitals and not let people bury their dead. It was natural to take advantage of that by re-introducing the famous queue and reminding people that Labour still wasn't working.

The first PEB on 19 April showed runners of different countries racing round a track with the British runners literally weighed down by tax/inflation burdens imposed by the Labour managers who were running the team that year. When the Conservative management took over – surprise, surprise – we beat even the Japanese. The second PEB, shown on 23 April, was in fact the only time that we used the crisis theme:

'Crisis, what crisis? . . . The things that make Britain great.'

In the second week of the campaign, we went into a press campaign. Our approach here was to try to cut through all the material coming at people from media experts about what the issues were, about who would win and what would happen if they did. We took a bold, factual approach to the issues, presenting on separate days Labour's record on crime, tax, unemployment and prices. We used the same approach in Lord Thorneycroft's PEB on 25 April and in the 'Educashun isn't wurking' poster which, together with a poster asking what Britain would be like in 1984 after another five years of Labour government, formed the basis of the poster campaign used in the second half of the election period.

The fourth PEB on 27 April was split between England/Wales and Scotland. The broadcast shown in England and Wales continued to develop the theme of Conservatism as commonsense. We simply posed the question, 'If you were a government, what would you do?' We tried to isolate the fact that Conservative proposals were in fact commonsense, the kinds of things that anyone with any sense would do whatever the party to which they belonged:

'What do you think should be done . . . Not because they're Conservative policies but because they're commonsense.'

The Scottish broadcast was written in the style of William McGonagall, a Scottish poet who wrote the worst rhyming poems of all time. At least in terms of its entertainment value, the broadcast was a huge success. Here's an extract from the seven minutes of contrived rhyme:

"Twas the disaster of '74 . . . if you want the end to be happy, you'd better vote Tory.'

In the last week of the campaign, we began to introduce the final slogan, 'It's time for a change'. As I've mentioned, this was not an original slogan. It's been used many times in many countries in many translations. But it's the classic slogan for capturing a national mood when people are in fact tired of a government. We tied the slogan in with the issues at which we had been hammering away throughout the campaign: unemployment, taxes and prices. Two days before polling day, we asked:

What are Labour policies? Labour policies have been made clear: more of the same. More of the same policies that doubled prices. More of the same policies that doubled unemployment. More of the same policies that doubled taxes. More of the same policies that left Britain in chaos and misery this winter. It's time for a change.

The day before polling day:

If five years ago before you voted you could have looked into the future and seen that Labour would double unemployment, double prices, double tax, would you have voted for them? It's time for a change.

And on polling day itself, 'It's time for a change'.

That, in brief, is the story of the campaign. Our contribution on its own did not win the campaign. In a sense, the Labour government lost the election by not holding it earlier. In May 1979 the campaign was taking place against the backdrop of the 'winter of discontent' and of Mrs Thatcher's broadcast at that time. Even before the winter of 1979–80, we had discovered that most people wanted an election. Mr Callaghan certainly did himself no favours at all by delaying the election.

Our summary of the campaign itself is that the government behaved like an opposition and the opposition behaved like the government. That too was a critical factor in determining the result. We were talking about something new, while they were talking about more of the same – and more of the same is not very appealing to people who feel that what they've got is not very good. We were helped, in addition, by an enormous amount of luck. In the build-up, for example, we had written the 'Cheer up! Labour can't hang on for ever' poster three months before the strikes during the winter of 1979–80. It was pure luck that we had that poster on the boards and ready to run.

But one effect our work certainly did have was, in advertising language, to stir up the sales force. The party workers were given some controversy to debate and argue about; they became active, mobile and self-confident. We said it was time for a change and a change there was.

Notes: Chapter 2

Tim Bell is Managing Director of Saatchi & Saatchi Advertising and led the advertising team advising the Conservatives in the 1979 general election.

1 Some of the Party Political Broadcasts quoted in this chapter are given at greater length in Appendix 1.
2 See Lord Windlesham, *Communication and Political Power* (London: Cape, 1966), p. 53.
3 These areas all included Labour marginals.

3

Labour's Advertising Campaign

TIM DELANEY

My discussion of Labour's advertising in the 1979 election falls into three main parts. Like Tim Bell, I will begin by describing the team we put together to help the party with its advertising work. I will then describe the strategy paper which the team submitted and worked to in the campaign. And I will conclude with some reflections of my own on the general relationship between the Labour Party and advertising agencies, particularly as affected by the arrival of Saatchi & Saatchi on the political scene. I'm not in complete agreement with the Labour Party's current view on that relationship – but more of that later.

The members of the group we formed in 1977 were all volunteers. That meant we were willing to work to the best of our abilities for as long and as hard as the party wanted. It did not mean we were amateurs. The team included Edward Booth-Clibborn, Chairman of the Designers and Art Directors Association of London, and Trevor Eke, Managing Director of Playtex Ltd. In addition, we included professional film makers, copy writers and art directors, who were all of the same high professional standard. As a result, we faced the problems which arose from the hypocrisy of the Labour Party towards advertising agencies. The speeches objecting to soap-powder advertising techniques did not help the morale of the people trying to work for the Labour Party. Yet we had seen Saatchi & Saatchi coming. We had said to the party: look, the name of the game has changed. You can no longer cut to a picture of a man at a lathe every time you talk about industrial relations or to an old-age pensioner every time you talk about a caring, sharing society. Those days have gone. You have got to start thinking about the approach used in Tory PPBs and you must borrow some of their techniques. At the very least, you must acknowledge that the Conservative broadcasts are going to condition people to expect different things from party political broadcasts.

Our strategy document reflected these assumptions about the changing style of political advertising in Britain. But the objective of the advertising was not particularly new: it was to concentrate the campaign effort on those issues which we believed would be decisive in the forthcoming election. This objective was not as vacuous as it might sound. We knew that the party wanted to reiterate *ad nauseam* that the sharing, caring Labour Party really does care about people. The social and welfare issue certainly was a Labour issue, but it was not an issue uppermost in people's minds. The central issue, we felt, was the management of the economy, a broad term encompassing employment, industrial relations, prices, taxation, investment and work incentives. We felt that we had a record to talk about in this whole area, at least in comparison with the performance of previous Conservative governments. Given too the loose, unplanned nature of the working situation, we felt it was important to try to structure the campaign so that a focus was kept on the crucial issues. In that kind of context, it is too easy for ministers to come along and say 'I think this is important' or 'I think that is important'.

Although we put this document to the Labour Party before the winter of 1979–80, there was no evidence that the issues changed after this time. If anything, the issue of economic management became even more important after the 'winter of discontent' than before it. At the time when we were preparing the document, however, we relied for research on the findings of a Gallup Poll about the most salient issues, taken in 1978. This indicates the limited access we had to the party's private and more up-to-date research.

The key voters were those who were inclined to vote Labour but were not so committed that they did not need to be pesuaded by convincing argument on the issues. These swing voters, it transpired, were the skilled workers – the C2s in advertising jargon. Here was a traditionally Labour group to which we felt we could make a dramatic appeal based on performance rather than patriotism. What we were selling, essentially, was an improved standard of living – and our objective was to convince the target audience that only by continuing with a Labour government could that improved standard of living be achieved. In making this case we intended to refer both to past performance and future programmes; to the government's success in managing the economy in the 1974–9 period and to its proposals to create jobs, stabilise prices and stimulate investment in productive industries in the future.

At the time when this document was being prepared, I was concerned about the analogy with the 1970 election. It seemed to me there was a very real danger that the factors which produced a Tory victory then might well do so again. The government straightens out the economy but then has to watch the electorate slip away as a result of the punishment the electorate has been put through. Saatchi &

Saatchi had quite correctly identified the public feeling that a change of government is needed after a period of self-sacrifice (even if only *perceived* self-sacrifice), and I felt very strongly that we had to take this problem on board in order to prevent it overcoming us again. I was interested to see whether we could turn this around; in the event, obviously, we could not.

We felt that the strategy, as we had outlined it, should be followed in all aspects of the national campaign. It had to encompass not only the posters and press advertisements, but also (and more controversially) the PPBs, speeches and other statements designed to secure the re-election of the Labour government. On the caring and sharing issue, for example, it needed to be demonstrated that the only reason the party could afford to care and share was that it managed and would continue to manage the economy successfully. Economic management was to be the core of the whole strategy.

The development of the strategy was one thing; its implementation quite another. One problem to which I've already referred was the lack of sympathy in the Labour Party for professional advertising people. Tim Bell had a one-horse race on the flat compared to the course of Beecher's Brooks we had to jump. Although the people with whom we dealt in Number 10 were sympathetic to a professional attitude, the same cannot unfortunately be said of Transport House. Even though Transport House likes to have advertising people around and uses them freely, there is and always has been a deep suspicion of professional advertising people there.

A second, perhaps related, problem was the lack of cohesion and planning in the Labour campaign. One example of this is the party election broadcasts (PEBs) themselves, which we did not succeed in wresting away from Transport House until several days after the date of the election had been announced. This meant that we had four broadcasts to do in as many weeks, whereas Saatchi & Saatchi already had all their PEBs in the can by then. One of the most unfortunate consequences of this was that people like David Owen and Shirley Williams who appeared in the broadcasts only had about twenty minutes to familiarise themselves with what they were going to say. I feel bad looking at these broadcasts now because our politicians appeared nervous by comparison with those on the Conservative broadcasts, where much more time was clearly spent with the politicians beforehand.

Another example of the lack of cohesion in Labour's campaign is the confusion over press advertisements. As Tim Bell has pointed out, it is very important that all the advertisements should be produced in the same style. Yet we were dealing with different sections of Transport House which were competing with us right up to the last minute. They would show us advertisements saying 'why don't we run this on Thursday?', when we thought we were running something else. And this was one of the major communication campaigns of the decade, perhaps of any decade. Whatever the internal politics may be, it seems to me ridiculous that the campaign should not be cohesive and well mounted. The lack of funds of which the party is always complaining makes the need for cohesion even greater. This lack of cohesion is one thing that has got to be changed.

Money was a third problem. The Conservative Party spent over £1·9 million on advertising and PPBs in the run-up and the campaign, compared with a figure of under £700,000 for the Labour Party.[1] Given this discrepancy, it is not surprising that Saatchi & Saatchi were setting the pace. They blitzed the press during the election campaign and had a presence for about eighteen months before that with posters, broadcasts and well-placed press advertisements. The freewheeling, hit-and-run approach they adopted created an atmosphere which made people consider not just Tory policies, but politics generally. Basically, they were running the show – and that was a function of money as much as good strategy.

We eventually produced the first four of the party's TV election broadcasts. The fifth and final PEB was Mr Callaghan talking head to camera at Number 10 and was shot by a television crew. In our approach to these broadcasts we unashamedly stole some of the techniques used in the Tory broadcasts, because we too felt that the talking-head syndrome had to go. We were lumbered to a certain extent, because we were dealing with ministers – though ministers are after all important figures of the day. But we tried to break up the presentation with visual devices and captions to make it more interesting.

At the end of the election, someone commented that the campaign had really been about the Tory manifesto. Looking back over our PEBs I am inclined to agree that we did spend an awful lot of time knocking the Tories. Every broadcast started with a knock against the Tories and continued in similar vein. What we were trying to do here was to clarify in people's minds what the Tories were really all about. We wove the broadcasts around the contrast between Conservative promises and Labour's performance. But it is true, I think, that nothing positive came out of our broadcasts, a failing which reflects the fact that a party in government really only has more of the same to offer. It's an interesting point that both major parties felt that the most effective strategy for their advertising was to criticise the other party.

For the future, the most important question the Labour Party has to ask is: how can we adapt to the changes in the nature of political communication introduced by Saatchi & Saatchi? The answer, I believe, is to employ an advertising agency. It is very important for

Labour Party officials to realise that what Saatchi & Saatchi have done for the Tories is not to sell them like soap-powder, but is rather to produce the cohesion needed, first, to create a professional communications strategy and then, secondly, to make it work. An advertising agency is paid to think about new ways of presenting ideas to people rather than manipulating them. Without a more professional approach in the Labour Party to problems of political communication, one party will be talking through Saatchi & Saatchi to the people while the other will basically be talking to itself.

Notes: Chapter 3

Tim Delaney is Creative Director of Leagas Delaney Advertising and was adviser and advertising consultant to the Labour Party in the 1979 general election.

1 See Michael Pinto–Duschinsky, 'What should be the cost of a vote?', *The Times* (10 March 1980).

The Advertisers: Discussion

Alan Clarke (Open University)
There seems to be a real structural difference between the Conservative Party and the Labour Party. It just seems so much easier for opinion pollsters and for advertising people to work with the Conservative Party (because it is a simpler organisation) than it is with the Labour Party. Given that committees are so embedded into the Labour Party's structure, can the Labour Party ever hope to make proper use of these political tools – advertising and polls?

Tim Delaney
I can't answer the question for them. I hope they can, because advertising in political communication is here to stay. It has been proved to be effective and you can only deny that by sticking your head in the sand. Committees aren't wrong just because they exist. Tim Bell and I deal with committees all the time in large companies, whether it is the board itself or marketing groups. So just because the Labour Party has got many committees that doesn't mean the party can't handle a professional approach. I think the attitude must come from the top, perhaps from a couple of individuals who are responsible for publicity. It would certainly help if they could avoid the Pearl Carr and Teddy Johnson act we were dealing with last time.

Tim Bell
Tim (Delaney) touched earlier on the difference between being in opposition and being in government, and that really is a hell of a difference. We are continuing to work for the Conservative Party now that they are in government, and it isn't as easy as it was in 1979 when they were in opposition. So this may help to explain a part of the contrast between Tim Delaney's and my experience. In addition, there are definitely intellectual and emotional problems about advertising within the Labour Party. They don't actually think it is a very good thing, they think it's a rather nasty thing which distorts and lies and cheats. Unless you change that attitude of mind and develop an awareness of the power of advertising, you won't get a real change. The party has to believe that these things are worth while and that they work.

Austin Mitchell, MP
Though Saatchi & Saatchi were taking full fees for dealing in half-truths, and dogged and serious though our broadcasts were, both campaigns were in fact paddling on the surface of very basic groundswells. The essence of the campaign was that Labour pulled back and the Conservatives didn't improve their position, so that telling the argument as we saw it, even in a dogged and serious way, seems to have benefited us much more than the advertising-oriented technique of Saatchi & Saatchi helped the Conservative Party.

   We are told that you are identified with the Conservative Party pretty totally. Do you feel that this has any effect on the credibility of your agency? This is a product which you can't control and which isn't constant. If that product now fails, will it reflect on the credibility of the agency which told those half-truths for it?

Tim Bell
I work for professional manufacturers who recognise the power, importance and persuasiveness of marketing methods and that such methods are the only way to expand business in a free-enterprise economy. Consequently, my political opinions do not seem to influence the way they regard the services of my agency. We have lost no billing from manufacturers as a result of working for the Conservative Party. If the Conservative government fails, I've no doubt I will be abused in the streets, in the bar and elsewhere, but it won't affect the agency because we are simply professionals doing a job. The other point I want to make relates to your opening comment. I have already said that I do think the Labour Party broadcasts were better than the Conservative Party broadcasts. This has got nothing to do with half-truths, but it simply reflects the fact that the Labour broadcasts judged the mood of the electorate better. They were more serious; they were more to the point; they had more gravitas in them than our work. We recognised what was wrong, and as the campaign continued, we changed the tonal quality of the work. It should be reassuring to those who don't like the idea of advertising that we advertising men have discovered that you can be *too* flippant in a general election situation. People do actually think an election is a rather important and serious affair. We were too flippant in our television work, though not in the press work. We almost certainly won the press war. If you believe our broadcasts contained half-truths, then you must go to the party managers and talk to them. What we do is present the policies which we are given by the party. We do not tell the party what policies to adopt; we simply present the facts that we're given.

Part Two

The Politicians

4

The Local Campaign, 1977–9

AUSTIN MITCHELL, MP

You'd expect a winning candidate to begin with a panegyric about his constituency, paying especial attention to its good sense in electing him. I've always viewed the candidate as being of no more than marginal importance, and I saw nothing in Grimsby, neither the 1977 by-election nor 1979 general election, to change that view. But I can comply with the general requirement. Grimsby demands more work than most but it is the perfect constituency. With an electorate of 67,041 at the by-election on 28 April 1977, it's reasonably sized and bang on the electoral quota – a blessed relief when I see the redistribution terrors of some of my colleagues. That population is also the population of the borough (or if you're pedantic, the non-metropolitan district) whose boundaries are the same as mine, so the constituency has a real identity. This and Grimsby's isolation, protected as we are by the inadequacies of British Rail and the prolonged delay in Britain's most postponed road, the M180 extension, give the town a local pride, a feeling of identity usually lacking in sprawling rural electorates and city seats which are effectively slices of nowhere. They also give it a warmth and a friendliness which are the reverse side of the isolation coin. Shortly after I was elected – and I'm sure by coincidence since it was a Conservative council – the town took back the title of Great Grimsby. It seems entirely appropriate.

Tony Crosland had a particular pride in being Grimsby's member of Parliament, probably because Grimsby is a slice of the real England, removed from metropolitan preoccupations and the impersonality of big cities, dominated by no group, having a wide range of occupations and interests. It has its own local issues but basically Grimsby responds to the national problems: jobs, houses, welfare, health, like a barometer for the nation. What workaday Britain thinks today, so does Grimsby.

Grimsby is still primarily a fishing port. This in turn supports what is now the country's most important fish market, an extensive distribution network and fish-processing plants run by Ross, Bird's Eye and Findus which have in turn diversified into food processing generally. The calculation is twelve jobs onshore for every one at sea. Originally, 50 per cent of the catch came from distant waters. The end of Icelandic fishing in 1976 put some 2,000 fishermen out of work, and caused the distant-water industry gradually to atrophy. Vessels were laid up on the North Wall, and the freezers transferred to Hull, so that by 1979 there were only just over a score, now a dozen, distant-water vessels left. Grimsby fought back well. Inshore fishing, seine netting and pair trawling have expanded, and in place of the eighty or so distant-water vessels, we soon had nearly 200 smaller ones catching perhaps 4,000 kits of fish a day in summer compared to the 12,000 or so when we worked in Icelandic waters. The decline was not as abrupt or disastrous as Hull. Yet the blow was still severe. It made fishing the major issue in both elections.

In both, my opponent, Robbie Blair, was a Bird's Eye executive. That job didn't help him; to be a big employer of local labour is a disadvantage, while the industry is hardly enamoured of a dominant influence on the market, yet he did know the industry backwards. I could claim only a local journalist's knowledge (which means not very much). So while fighting the by-election campaign, I was doing an adult-education course on fishing by talking to anyone who could help and reading everything I could get which was mainly material supplied by John Silkin's office.

As the biggest town for a fifty-mile radius (until the Humber Bridge – which we're not keen on – is completed), Grimsby is a natural focus for services and shopping for a large, and under the Common Agricultural Policy increasingly prosperous, rural area. Moreover thanks to the far-sighted efforts of Grimsby Council since the war, it has diversified by bringing in engineering, mostly small-scale though there is also the Humber Graving Dock, textiles in the form of a massive Courtaulds artificial-fibre plant, chemicals in Laportes and British Titan, Fisons, oil refining and, as mentioned earlier, food processing. Most of this industry is outside the town on the Humber bank, so Grimsby is somewhere to live in, work is somewhere else, except for the food processing which mainly employs women and gives the town a characteristic which became important. It is a low-wage area, compared to, say, mining areas or the midlands car industry. Its feelings about incomes policy were very different to theirs.

Grimsby has always been a marginal seat. Labour first won it in 1945 and held it in 1950, when the neighbouring and much more Tory town of Cleethorpes was split away, coming to its narrowest victory in 1959, when Tony Crosland was first elected by 101 votes. From then he was never really threatened, having a majority of 8·6 per cent in 1964, 17·8 per cent in 1966, 13·6 per cent in 1970, 11·2 per cent in February 1974 and 15·2 per cent in October.

Between 1974 and the 1979 election the by-election intervened. The 1979 general election can't really be understood without considering the by-election first. It was a repeat match for the two main candidates, fighting much the same issues on the same ground but to a very different result. Tony Crosland died in February 1977. I was considering standing for selection (though not very actively because of the disaster of my two previous attempts at selection, and the repercussions on my job as a journalist/presenter at Yorkshire Television) when an invitation from a senior member of the Grimsby party clinched it. The selection was held, perhaps appropriately, on 1 April, the day after the Stechford disaster. Keith Kyle, one of the other short-listees, kept making jokes about who would have the poisoned chalice. We all laughed nervously and it was such a high-powered list that some of the others understood. I got the chalice. Much to my surprise. My job at Yorkshire finished the next day. I don't think I've ever felt more lost and miserable.

These feelings vanished once the campaign began, four days later. A by-election campaign has powerful momentum. The candidate is just the figurehead for the national party, for the full-time professionals move in but the puppet's feet don't even touch the ground. Time to think is the worst problem. You've got to write your speeches, think out your policies, swot up on the issues, write your pamphlets and press releases all while on the go. A performing chimpanzee can fight a general election. In a by-election, with national media coverage and the candidate strutting, sometimes fretting, on a much wider stage, he has to be a thinking chimpanzee, though the same physique will do because both are outward-bound courses.

Pressure keeps your mind off your worries, or anything else, but more important in dispelling my initial fears was the feedback from party and constituency. I'd begun by thinking I would lose. The media agreed. As soon as the campaign began, I thought I could win. Partly because Percy Clark the Labour Party Press Officer showed me a MORI poll the party had commissioned. This indicated that Grimsby could be won and that there was not that bitter hostility to the government which had characterised other by-elections. I was shown this poll and pledged to secrecy. It certainly cheered me up as did the wider response: a lot of grumbling but no real antagonism, and an underlying feeling that though they weren't doing particularly well, the government were doing their best in a very difficult situation and should be given a fair go.

Why did I scrape home by 520 votes? Some put it down to my being on television. Personally, I discount this. It was a help: the main job in a by-election is to get a candidate and a name known in three weeks. I had a big advantage here even over an opponent who was well known locally. It broke psychological barriers. I find glad-handing and imposing myself on people a nervous ordeal but in recognising me voters were half coming towards me. Yet I don't think this had much influence on the actual result. In some ways it had to be lived down. People expect their politicians to be politicians not glamour figures or stand-up comedians. Knowing me made them curious but I certainly had to prove myself to be a serious candidate.

Nor was it the Common Market. I was anti-Market, my opponent pro. Most of those members of Parliament who came to help were anti-Market. The Common Market was certainly important both in the fishing issue, where the industry was beginning to understand what a disaster the Common Market was for them, and more generally. Yet it was an issue I stumbled across rather than developed and exploited. There weren't a lot of questions on it, in fact getting Grimsby out of Humberside produced more feeling than getting Britain out of Europe. Its main importance was psychological. It put me on the attack in an election when defensiveness was almost predestined.

We held the seat because Grimsby was marginal. That concentrated minds on the real issue: did people want the government out? The previous member was well respected and had died in office, not gone off to make money in Europe. As it turned out, the tide, running strongly against the government through the earlier months, was turning and Grimsby was the hinge. Turnout was up, rare in a by-election, and our whole strategy had been to get our people out, knowing they would vote for us if they voted at all.

Winning set the scene for a general election victory. If Grimsby could be held in the climate of early 1977, it could be held when support began to return to the government. More important, the by-election victory welded together and enthused a local party which was delighted to have held the seat. We are only a small party (with less than 300 members at the time of the by-election) but few local parties can have been as united, as active and as enthusiastic. Victory is a psychological booster.

The general election was a complete contrast to 1977. At the general election you're on your own. Just you and the local party. Transport House promised help but neither of the two visiting speakers they arranged turned up. John Silkin and Roy Hattersley both came to speak for me, but they did so as personal favours at my request. Nor did the trade union Campaign For a Labour Victory provide much. The promised organiser never came and though twenty dockers did come down from Hull for a day, they arrived on a Hull corporation bus which drove round the town for much of the afternoon, snarling up the traffic and exacerbating the very real anti-Hull feeling in Grimsby. The organisation work fell mainly on my agent, a school dentist who continued to work through most of the campaign (indeed, at one stage he had to treat me), and my secretary, who I found to my dismay had to be paid by me for the campaign period. With the backing of the local party, they coped superbly. The fact that the general election and the election of the entire borough council were on the same day guaranteed that a major workforce of thirty-six would-be councillors, their families and friends would be out working hard for their future and mine. All that we lacked was money and here we received an enormous boost in the middle of the campaign, a cheque for £1,000 from the boilermakers which saved our bacon and averted what would otherwise have been a financial disaster.

A by-election is about politics. General elections in the constituency are about people. The local candidate is an intruder on the national campaign, knocking on doors and interrupting television watching or newspaper reading. Instead of creating the issues as we'd tried to do at the by-election, you're responding to those being argued nationally. With the most moderate, not to say innocuous manifesto we've ever had, the issue I had to respond to most was the reds-under-the-beds one, or Tony Benn's remorseless drive to power and the threat from union militants. These were supplemented by the local report that my wife is Arthur Scargill's sister, the 1979 equivalent of the by-election whispering campaign that I was a Yorkie standing for a Yellowbelly seat, a view which had been assiduously propagated by a team of lady canvassers brought in from Harrogate. I felt that the left-wing take-over issue was usually raised by people who were seeking an excuse for not voting Labour or rationalising a decision they were hovering over, but there is no doubt in my mind that it provided the biggest single local feedback from the national campaign.

At a by-election, given the massive media interest, you have few problems in reaching people, even if most of them are outside Grimsby. In a general election you pound the streets looking for them. The local paper, the *Grimsby Evening Telegraph*, remained studiously impartial, devoting absolutely equal coverage (as measured in inches) to each side, carrying nothing else. Yorkshire Television did even less than its duty, failing to carry any of the stories I so assiduously sent them. Radio Humberside was kinder. Yet in every case a candidate is left with the uneasy feeling that even if he dropped dead in the street it wouldn't be mentioned if his opponent wasn't doing anything usable that day. To get round this frustrating feeling of being encased in Dunlopillo, I accepted every invitation to a collective meeting offered (only two were) and had as many public meetings as possible to put the issues to the people. I also carried on a campaign of maximum visibility, canvassing in different wards each morning, afternoon or evening, visiting factories (if they'd have me which most wouldn't), leafleting factory gates, going out with the speaker car, constantly being out and about to be seen by and meet as many people as possible.

This is the outward-bound aspect. The basic problem is the simple one of physical survival: fighting off the strain, keeping your temper and keeping smiling. Nerves do become very frayed as a result defending things you feel strongly about, responding to attacks and criticisms (which always seem malevolent and personal), and hearing constant rumours of what Tory canvassers have been saying on the doorstep. Yet it's vital to avoid hurt or anger. I nearly broke when a maverick Labour man arrived from Hull and for no very clear reason set himself up as a Moderate Labour Party candidate. I was all for a writ to stop the use of the words 'Labour Party', fearing the intervention could be crucial in a close result (as it probably would have been given the number of voters who spoilt their ballots by voting for both Labour men). My agent remained cool and far more sensible, and he was quite right.

Though the main aim of the campaign was irrational, to put a personality on the national campaign and to give a face to the party, I tried hard to keep a rational thread to it. I felt very strongly that the Labour government had done a reasonable job in very difficult circumstances, that it had been unfairly blamed for things beyond its control, that the Tory alternative was dangerous, unworkable and would be positively harmful if applied. I put this argument as widely as possible in the meetings, in the media when allowed to do so and through a series of cyclostyled yellow fact sheets which we distributed as widely as possible through party members and union contacts, and which evidently got home. My opponent called them 'the yellow press'. Yet strongly as I felt about the gospel, I would doubt whether it directly affected more than 500–600 people. What effect the printed word had, I can't judge.

The strength of my feeling came from the unfair deal I thought the Labour government had had and the confidence trick which I felt the Conservatives were pulling on the people. It was a simple-minded line but mine own. The only help I got in elaborating it came from the party's speech-notes which were rather too detailed to be usable and the daily diet of facts in the cyclostyled *Today* sheets. These seemed to arrive in Grimsby a day after elsewhere but were still very useful in providing ammunition. Not all of it worked. Using the information about prices, I prepared a news release on the effect of Tory devaluation of the 'green pound' on the average shopping basket and Radio Humberside carried it. Next day came a correction from Transport House. The figures were wrong.

Because the job of explanation was such an uphill one, because of the constant nagging feeling that we weren't reaching the people, because our national campaign seemed so flat, I didn't enjoy the election campaign. A by-election is an experience. Win or lose, I wouldn't have missed mine. A general election is a duty. It puts your feet on the ground. It brings you back to basic realities. It revitalises that osmosis which should be going on all the time. Yet basically it's frustrating. The ordinary candidate has so much to say and so little impact. He works frantically but in the end is elected or rejected because of reactions to a government he scarcely influences and a national campaign of which he's not even a part. The situation is rather like being locked in a vandalised phone-box while a battle rages outside.

The frustration ended at 10 o'clock on 3 May. I couldn't really take the local count in, sitting downstairs morosely watching on the television the depressing roll-call of good friends and good members thrown out for no good reason. Nevertheless, the final result is given in Table 4.1.

Table 4.1

	BY-ELECTION	
A. V. Mitchell (Labour)	21,890	(46·9%)
R. Blair (Conservative)	21,370	(45·8%)
A. De Freitas (Liberal)	3,128	(6·7%)
M. Stanton (Socialist Worker)	215	(0·5%)
P. H. H. Bishop (Sunshine)	64	(0·1%)
M. Nottingham (Malcolm Muggeridge Fan Club)	30	(0·06%)
	GENERAL ELECTION	
A. V. Mitchell (Labour)	26,282	(52·0%)
R. Blair (Conservative)	20,041	(39·7%)
D. M. Rigby (Liberal)	3,837	(7·6%)
J. Lennard (Moderate Labour)	214	(0·4%)
J. Hayes (National Front)	137	(0·3%)

Note:
Electorate at by-election: 67,041.
Electorate at general election: 66,644.

A massive swing since the by-election; basically Grimsby had merely reverted to the pattern it had disturbed, for the result was very similar to that which could have been expected had Tony Crosland lived. Perhaps that was a greater achievement for me than winning the by-election.

Note: Chapter 4

Austin Mitchell, MP (Labour), sits for Grimsby and is a journalist and former television newscaster.

5

Political Communications in the 1979 General Election Campaign by One Who Was In It

TIM RATHBONE, MP

The Conservative election campaign in 1979 was professionally planned and executed; perhaps it was the most professional Conservative campaign ever. The party hierarchy was aware of the need for professional research (both quantitative and qualitative), for proper analysis of that research and for sophisticated use of the information so gained in the planning and execution of the pre-election and election political propaganda. Whatever the effect of planned political communications in previous elections, the effect on behalf of the Conservatives in 1979 must have been considerable.

This should not be taken to intimate that policy was based upon populist market-research findings; that, I suggest, is the way to lose elections not to win them. Rather, once policy direction was agreed, the party could measure and carefully analyse the electoral appeal of the various policy directions and then, better than ever before, activate party political propaganda to make the best of them.

But that is not all. The process of analysis must have reinforced the party leader's own instinctive feeling for the need to re-state Conservative Party principles as well as policies. I have to presume, on the basis of the success of that re-statement, that the exercise in propaganda planning would also have identified the various directions into which such principles could be most easily and effectively communicated.

While this process was not in complete contrast to previous election campaigns, the degree of importance attached to it appears to have been almost unique. When I was head of publicity at Conservative Central Office, in the mid-1960s, the need for research became well appreciated. But the use of research findings then was sadly proscribed by suspicion of the whole activity and of the people involved in it. This was true in 1970 and I believe that it was true also in 1974. By 1979 the party had overcome these suspicions; and, as well as appreciating the need for communication professionals in campaign planning and execution, there seems to have been a determined effort to appreciate and to use their professional skills. Also, and this is very important, those professionals could not have been as successful as they undoubtedly were if this determination and appreciation had not stretched through all the layers of Central Office, to the leader's office, and to the leader herself.

At last the Conservative Party was prepared to seek out people of calibre in the communications world and expect them to make an important contribution to the Conservative election campaign thrust. Gordon Reece was just one of those people, combining as he did extremely effective public-relations instincts with a wealth of television experience. I have to admit a bias towards Gordon, in that he produced the very first party political broadcast for which I was responsible in 1966. He was effective then, but even more so in 1978 and 1979. But, as I have intimated already, it would be true to say that his more recent effectiveness was dependent as much upon his relationship with the leader of the party as upon his own professional talents. He must have been looked upon by her as being completely reasonable and trustworthy – as well as being professionally talented.

Then, also, the party's advertising agency, Saatchi & Saatchi, was also treated in a professional way. Chosen largely because of its undoubted creative talent but also because of the dedication to the Conservative cause of its then Managing Director, Tim Bell, it was brought in for consultations early in the planning process and at the highest level; and it too was given ready access to the chairman of the party and to the leader. Having understood what needed doing it was, furthermore, allowed to get on with the job in a way which had probably never existed before. It, therefore, was able to plan advertising and broadcasts which would make contact with and persuade very specific audiences because they understood, as all professional advertising men understand, that this is the best way to use the communications methods available to the party, to best effect. So, applying this principle to the use of political posters, much of the poster campaign which ran before and during the election was concentrated in the marginal constituencies where their effect was needed the most. But perhaps the most notable example of specific targeting of a political message was in the use of a cinema commercial directed to the young people who make up the majority of any cinema audience; this, unusually for any commercial, could almost always be guaranteed to elicit from the young people in the audience a most positive reaction of sympathetic amusement and applause – an expression which only went to underline the understanding and the credibility of the message which the commercial was attempting to convey.

There is little doubt that the party's advertising activities were designed 'to touch existing raw nerve ends', for instance, fear of even more left-wing government, fear of unemployment, fear of national bankruptcy. In doing this it did what advertising does best, which is to embellish and to strengthen existing beliefs. And this it did very well.

But whatever peripheral activities were mounted, and whatever their success, the real election battle was fought through leadership projection on television. Indeed, television coverage whether by way of party political broadcasts or by news report, was the essence of the election campaign. In this, as in the advertising campaign, the task facing the Conservative Party in opposing the then existing Labour government was made that much easier, because it was essentially the Conservatives' task to argue for change when there was already an established predisposition among the electorate for that change. The people had made up their minds that they were worried; they had made up their minds that they wanted something done about it; so it was only thereafter necessary to confirm their worry and to nudge them along towards taking the action needed to bring about such a change – by voting Conservative.

To be successful in these circumstances, party political communications, particularly through television, were not and did not essentially have to be factual communications. Rather their major task and, in that election, their major success was to reinforce Conservative ideology and contrast that with the ideology of the left. That is not to argue against the use of fact as supporting data for political communication; rather it is an attempt to explain the true effect of television communication and to put it in the right context, especially as it pertained to the political world of 1979.

Of course, most if not all of the national television coverage goes on unseen by the local candidate. But that is not the only way in which a candidate finds himself in a peculiar role. During an election campaign, a constituency candidate is really very cut off from the rest of the country. This was particularly the case in the last election, because fighting the electoral battle in the generally strong Conservative south-east seemed to be a far cry from the industrial Midlands and the north. Even so, though removed from the rest of the country, the arguments in the local constituency, in my experience, are almost totally to do with national issues and have very little bearing on local politics. This is in contrast to the times between elections when so much of a member of Parliament's time in surgeries and at meetings is taken up with local matters.

Much is made of the fact that any candidate has only marginal effect on the outcome in any single constituency; however hurtful that is to one's own personal pride, the point has to be accepted more now than ever before. That in turn raises a question about what might be considered to be the illogicality of much of the activities of a constituency candidate at election time. Indeed, some of the changes in election campaign practice reflect such a conclusion. For instance, in the Lewes constituency it is no longer the practice to have a grand end-of-campaign, eve-of-poll meeting. It is considered far more valuable to have supporters finishing their canvass calls, so that their polling-day follow-up can be the better organised, than it is to attempt to attract them to a final political rally. It must also be said that constituency election meetings are less important than before the advent of television, though this may be more the case in those areas of the country where local newspapers are published weekly. The message of most meetings, after all, can only effect those people who attend the meeting.

But there are other bases for hypothesising that the campaigning activities of a local candidate are somewhat illogical. It must, for instance, be open to question whether the series of personal contact activities through canvassing door-to-door, talking to people on their way to and from work, and soapbox meetings in precincts during a shopping day, really have the effect of persuading people to vote as the candidate would wish. Undoubtedly, these activities, as well as the less personal communications through use of a car loudspeaker or the political dressing of a car and its entourage, all contribute to the vitality of the election campaign and most certainly make some contribution to maintaining the morale of one's own supporters and helpers. But the real reason for these activities, the hullaballoo of electioneering, is that they are seen to be part and parcel of an election campaign and that, by and large, they are enjoyed by candidates themselves. They are undertaken, it would appear, more in a spirit of electoral ebullience than with serious thought as to the need for them or the efficacy of them. But election campaigns would be the drabber without them.[1]

I sometimes wonder also whether the various forms of direct written communication cannot be as easily questioned, in terms of electoral efficacy. A candidate's introductory leaflet, which nowadays is often designed to act as a window-sticker as well, and the election address, the candidate's major message to every household in the constituency, certainly have some influence in building greater knowledge of a candidate, his character and, perhaps, some of his more idiosyncratic political beliefs. But I very much doubt whether they have a very great direct effect on the outcome of the constituency campaign. Rather, I believe their major contribution is to be seen as reinforcing the national publicity campaign. To that extent it is important to have this material, as well as name-identification posters and other election propaganda, so designed as to be seen as part of the national effort. Conservative Central Office certainly sets considerable importance on achieving this and, in spite of some continuing local variations in colour identification (and in almost everything else in one place or another), they are right to do so and have done so to quite good effect. I certainly set considerable store in carrying the national message and the national campaign slogan in as much of my own campaign material as possible.

The activities undertaken in an election campaign undoubtedly provide an opportunity for a candidate (even when he has been the sitting member of Parliament) to increase his visibility within the constituency. And this is even the case among his own party supporters. Indeed, it is arguable that the effect of election campaign activities is mostly felt in terms of the candidate's standing among his own party's supporters. This is marked in many of the activities but nowhere more dramatically than in the election day tour of committee rooms which has much to do with saying well-done and thank-you to all of those who have worked hard for you during the campaign, but has little relevance to the actual outcome of that campaign, except in the most marginal seats where the extra supporters reminded to vote or helped to the polls by those manning the committee rooms can make all the difference to the outcome. But, whether entirely effective or not, such an activity is pleasant and stimulating (like much of an election campaign) even though, in this particular instance, it is also the start of what is always a very long day.

I have mentioned the very considerable effect of national television, but there is also, for the party nationally and for candidates locally, the effect of local media. Here one must remark on the increasing effect of radio. Locally, in the Lewes constituency, I have coverage from Radio Brighton, a local BBC radio station which covers almost all of my constituency and is an increasingly useful and effective medium for news reporting. Unfortunately, in the 1979 election, their local effect was confined to news reporting because I had no opportunity of speaking, since the rules of political broadcasting require that all candidates are given equal time. One of my opposing candidates refused to co-operate and that removed the opportunity from all of the others. It seems to me that equality of opportunity to broadcast is a quite correct principle; but if, in an election campaign, one candidate refuses such an opportunity, then the others should be allowed to broadcast anyway. Otherwise the principle of balance becomes a sham – and that is a shame.

In parentheses, I should mention that when canvassing and at meetings the radio was mentioned to me more often than any other single medium, and this I believe can be traced to the increased number of call-in programmes, when party spokesmen expose themselves to challenge and questioning. It is therefore not surprising that this influence through national radio has increased, because such opportunities must be welcomed by those who participate – and by those who listen in. It is, I believe, an interesting and worthwhile innovation in political communications.

In the Lewes constituency local newspapers do not play an extremely important part in election communications. There are three weekly newspapers, each covering a part of the constituency but each overlapping with another. In essence, each only has one issue which is an election issue, and that appears towards the end of the middle week of an election campaign. Coverage of the politics of the campaign is generally confined to statements of 200–250 words from each candidate, and a situation report on the local campaign. Even within their own self-imposed publishing deadlines, it seems to me to be a pity that such important local media do not provide more information about the candidates in their total circulation area; too often the gimmick photograph is the only point of interest – and that is sometimes only too obviously contrived. I presume, of course, that they would quickly report any serious disagreement with the leadership of one's own party, since this would be 'news scoop'. But I would still like to see more reports, in weekly newspapers, of each candidate's personal emphasis or interpretation of his own party's policies and his own criticisms of those policies offered by opposing parties. This I would see as a service to local newspaper readers which many of them can get in no other way.

As the importance of the local newspaper has diminished, so the importance of direct mail has grown. I have already mentioned the election address, that classic and most important piece of direct mail which goes through the Freepost to every household in the constituency. Whatever the effect of this communication in the past, I think it is going to increase in importance in the future. Indeed, in some countries the correct use of direct mail in elections can be crucial, and I know of at least one instance where a completely unknown candidate launched himself successfully and won his election entirely through the use of sophisticated, personalised direct-mail communications to every influential elector in his constituency. This is expensive, of course. But if ever there is a revolution against influence from 'the centre' or an increase in the absolute influence of the local candidate, then direct mail would have an increasingly important and effective part to play in election campaigns here.

One way of avoiding the cost of direct mail is through direct delivery for which, of course, you have to depend on the enthusiasm and energy of your own party's supporters. Introductory leaflets are delivered in this way; and many personalised poster displays are achieved by direct delivery of the display material and, often, direct help in getting it put up on display. Whatever the effect on electors (and the cumulative effect may be greater than we think), it is immensely reassuring to the candidate and his supporters to wander about and find that he is known and is 'on display' – hopefully more than his opponents may be.

In many areas, and certainly in Sussex which is a generally Conservative county by inclination, it is possible to build up an effective look-alike Conservative campaign on behalf of the party and of each and all of the candidates in the area, by using centrally produced posters with the same design treatment on which only the name of the individual candidate is changed. This carries through into poster displays too.

By way of conclusion, it is worth re-emphasising the reality of the great divide between the national campaign waged through the national media from 'the political party centres' and the local campaigns waged by local candidates on the trot round their constituencies. I certainly have found that the national campaign has had little direct effect on the character of my own. Even though the briefing materials provided from the centre by Conservative Central Office have always proved extremely useful, the evolving national campaign often seems to be a thing apart. This must largely derive from the omnipresence of the television debate for everyone except candidates themselves, who alone seldom seem to have the opportunity to watch election television programming. It may be also that there is a greater unstated awareness among all candidates in our present electoral system, in that they in fact know and accept their own relative impotency in influencing the outcome of their own campaign. However that may be, the fact of the campaign, national and local, is an essential component of our democratic process; and anybody who doesn't like campaigning perhaps shouldn't be in politics in the first place.

Notes: Chapter 5

Tim Rathbone, MP (Conservative) sits for Lewes, Sussex, and is a director of the Charles Barker Group, advertising and public relations, and was formerly head of publicity for Conservative Central Office.

1 See, for example, J. Bochel and D. Denver, 'Canvassing, turnout and party support', *British Journal of Political Science*, vol. I (1971), pp. 257–69.

The Politicians: Discussion

Peter Kellner (Sunday Times)
Did you feel being out campaigning you were missing out on the national campaign that your constituents were experiencing through television? Secondly, both parties devoted much effort to pumping out enormous amounts of material to candidates and agents in each constituency; what use, if any, did either of you make of that material?

Tim Rathbone
I was absolutely cut off from the television campaign. However, it was interesting that the television campaign did not seem to generate questions at the meetings or during canvassing. I did not feel specifically divorced from the national campaign, except in so far that the south of England was divorced from the Midlands and the north of England. That was somehow an uncomfortable feeling for me. The centrally produced material was immensely valuable up to the start of the election campaign. It was copious and well-produced briefing material. After that, there just was not enough time to digest the material. The only way I used the material during the campaign was to answer specific queries from one of the single-issue groups that sent in questionnaires or letters.

Austin Mitchell
I saw practically nothing of the national campaign. This was probably an advantage, in that it forced me to press on with the local campaign and the issues which I thought important rather than responding in random fashion to the national campaign. On the second question, we, like the Tories, received a lot of material from Head Office. It was much better than usual for the Labour Party. However, in contrast to Tim Rathbone, I found the material was most useful during the campaign itself. You really don't have much time to think during the campaign; you need predigested intellectual material. Although we seemed to get *Today* a day later than everybody else, it did contain very useful debating points: what would be the effect of this Tory policy? What would be the effect, if this job support scheme were cut? These points were very effective for the kind of campaign I was fighting. The only time the material came to grief was on one occasion when there was a calculation about the effect of a devaluation of the 'green pound' on food prices. So I went out and did an elaborate exercise: 'Austin Mitchell today went shopping to show the effect of a devaluation of the green pound on the price of butter.' Radio Humberside obligingly carried the lot and then next day a new edition of *Today* arrived with a special correction and an instruction to ignore previous figures. But that was the only time it came to grief.

Bruce Page (New Statesman)
On the canvassing issue: I have done quite a lot of canvassing myself as a foot soldier, not as a candidate. It never crossed my mind for one instant that it had

any effect whatsoever. One does it purely because the ethos of the Labour Party requires that its members should do it to show that they are good souls. I don't entirely scorn that. I think it is perhaps proper that the party should make demands of its members. Certainly, one way of discovering whether you believe in a party is to stand in the rain outside a municipal block at 8 p.m. and wonder if you feel like knocking on a couple more doors. But the idea that this swings any votes whatsoever is to me a total illusion – and a dangerous one at that because most of the party's energy goes into it, when in fact our energy should go into policy formation before the election. I am certain that what happens in campaigns at any level doesn't make much difference unless the leader of one of the parties is caught drunk on television, and I doubt whether that would make much difference anyway. As an exercise in political conversion, canvassing is and must be useless. If two or three minutes conversation with an unbriefed party worker in the evening when the member of the public wants to get on with something else could swing votes, the people of Britain would be political morons. Which they clearly aren't.

Austin Mitchell
I wouldn't advance canvassing as a means of converting people. It's simply a way of putting a human face on the party. In a sense, it's the elector's right.

Bruce Page
I would go further and say that the fantasy about dragging out the votes which we go through on election night is equally a waste of energy which may in fact antagonise a number of people. People say to themselves: 'I'm not going to have some idiot banging on my door trying to drag me off to the polls.' I have visited our local ward in local elections to see whether there is any correlation whatsoever between activism and turnout. There is zilch.

John Bochel (University of Dundee)
I'm afraid that demonstrates a complete misconception about the purpose of canvassing in the Labour Party. Nobody pretends that you canvass in order to convert people, nor, I'm afraid, do you canvass in order to put a human face on politics. It's a way of getting people to vote.

Austin Mitchell
From the candidate's point of view, I do think canvassing is useful in getting out the vote on the day. Think of a situation without canvassing in which the party hasn't approached people. Electors wouldn't know who their candidate is: the party could be dead for all they know. Surely, that would make a difference?

Ivor Crewe (University of Essex)
There is a great deal of research on this issue which shows quite clearly on the basis of systematic experimental evidence that in *local* elections where turnout is normally low, the effect of extensive canvassing concentrated in a particular ward or a particular part of the constituency does increase turnout.

Bob Worcester (MORI)
It is not fair really to bring in evidence from a local election, where half the people don't know the election is taking place until they are knocked up, and then to extrapolate that to a national election, where people do know what is going on.

Tim Rathbone
In my own constituency (and I don't think you can generalise from Lewes any more than from Islington) people miss it, if they are not knocked up. They actually call in and ask for lifts, if they have been promised them. Knocking up is an absolutely imperative part of giving party workers something to do. Don't rule that out; it's very important.

Jack Brand (University of Strathclyde)
I was intrigued to hear Tim Rathbone say that he was rather sceptical about the effect of a candidate's activity during the campaign, implying none the less that pre-campaign activity by the candidate was rather more important. Can I ask him to expand on that?

Tim Rathbone
I was really talking about my own personal instance. During your time as a Member of Parliament, you build up public awareness and develop a political identity in the constituency. This results from your behaviour in, your presence at, and your commitment to, the everyday process of fete openings. The other theory was that the coincidence of the two elections would increase turnout in the local elections and thereby help the Labour Party. The second theory didn't prove to be accurate in Lewes but I honestly don't know what the form was nationally. I think I got more support from the district candidates than would otherwise have been the case. Similarly, I was able to give the local candidates more support than if the district council elections had just been going on in their own sweet time.

Peter Pulzer (Christ Church, Oxford), Chairman
How do we explain the apparently endemic difference in the quality of Labour and Conservative organisation in this country? From what we have heard at this conference, it seems remarkable that the Labour Party has won four out of the last six general elections. Now, one explanation is that the Labour Party lacks an instinct for public relations; it's a party which by the very nature of its composition doesn't rate the smooth running of an operation very highly. I'm sceptical of this explanation. For one thing, the Labour Party does in fact contain a large number of people who do possess managerial skills, or at least who ought to do so in view of their job or their education. In any case, the European experience does show that, now and historically, it is the working-class parties which are the best organised. It is the communist parties which pioneered the modern political machine, with its bureaucracy and ancillary organisations. So one has to find the explanation somewhere else. I would suggest that it has to do with the radical temperament in British politics to which a part of the Labour Party is heir. This temperament is distrustful of

paternalism, distrustful of efficiency for efficiency's sake, distrustful of the mechanisation of any aspect of human life but particularly of government and the formation of public opinion. I would, therefore, like to leave you with the thought that the Labour Party is saddled with vices which might in other contexts be considered virtues.

Part Three

The Media

6

Electoral Perceptions of Media Stance

PETER KELLNER and ROBERT M. WORCESTER

Much has been written about newspaper and radio and television coverage of general elections but little is known about the views of their customers – the readers, viewers and listeners. During the 1979 general election, the *Sunday Times* commissioned MORI to undertake a four-wave panel study. (Because publication at Times Newspapers had been suspended, and a planned resumption on 17 April had not taken place, some of the findings were reported in the *New Statesman* on 27 April and 4 May.) In the course of the questionnaire, MORI asked:

(1) Thinking about the election coverage you've seen in the news-papers so far, do you think this has been biased towards the Conservatives' point of view, towards Labour's point of view, or do you feel their coverage has been unbiased?

(2) Do you feel the radio has been biased towards the Conservatives' point of view, towards Labour's point of view, or do you feel their coverage has been unbiased?

(3) And thinking about the election coverage you've seen on BBC television. Do you think this has been biased towards the Conservatives' point of view, towards Labour's point of view, or do you feel their coverage has been unbiased?

(4) And finally the ITV election coverage. Has this been biased towards the Conservatives' point of view, Labour's point of view, or has it been unbiased?

The results were as in Table 6.1.

Two main points emerge: first, very few people considered the broadcasting media biased in 1979, although there is a slight indication of a lingering 'establishment' image for the BBC, with the minority believing it to be biased towards the Conservatives (9 per cent), twice as high as those believing it to be biased towards Labour (4 per cent). This is a significant improvement on the record of 1974,

Table 6.1   *Media Bias*

	Newspapers (%)	Radio (%)	Television BBC (%)	ITV (%)
Biased Tory	24	3	9	4
Biased Labour	10	2	4	4
Unbiased	35	44	70	71
DK	31	52	18	21

Source:
MORI (*Sunday Times*).
FW: 17–19 April 1979.

when 17 per cent thought the BBC biased according to an NOP poll (8 per cent thought ITV biased). Secondly, Conservative bias in the press was considerably more keenly felt than Labour bias; yet two-thirds of the sample either detected no newspaper bias, or didn't know. MORI analysed the question about newspaper bias by the newspaper each of the sample read. These are the responses for the five most widely read daily newspapers (for the other papers the sub-sample was too small for analysis) (Table 6.2).

Table 6.2   *Media Bias*

	Biased Tory (%)	Biased Labour (%)	Unbiased/ DK (%)
Daily Mirror	24	19	56
Sun	28	9	63
Daily Express	44	5	52
Daily Mail	45	9	46
Daily Telegraph	41	2	57

Some caveats must be entered. We asked about general perceptions of press bias, not separately about the bias of each newspaper. And a considerable minority either take more than one paper regularly, or see more than one paper occasionally. So the figure for the *Daily Mirror*, for example, may reflect in part a general feeling among some of its readers that the press as a whole is anti-Labour, rather than the *Mirror* itself. But it is also probable that the *Mirror*'s hostile stance towards a number of strikes the previous winter – and many of the strikers would have been *Mirror* readers – diluted the paper's image as a steadfast ally of the working class.

Conservative bias in the press was more widely perceived among Conservative supporters (26 per cent) than among Labour supporters (19 per cent). This apparently paradoxical finding – Tory bias is generally a Labour complaint – is largely explained by the fact that most Conservative voters read Conservative papers, while most Labour voters read either the Labour *Daily Mirror*, or the ex-Labour *Sun* (Tables 6.3 and 6.4). The *Telegraph* dropped from a net 58 per cent Tory readership in 1978 to a 47 per cent level after the election. (See Tables 6.5 and 6.6.)

Table 6.3 *Election Readership*

(*n* =)	All Electors (1,824) (%)	*Daily Express* (280) (%)	*Daily Mail* (235) (%)	*Daily Mirror* (210) (%)	*Sun* (396) (%)	*Daily Telegraph* (160) (%)
Conservative	45	65	67	21	38	73
Labour	40	22	23	64	52	15
Liberal	12	10	9	9	9	11
Other	2	3	1	5	2	1
Conservative Lead	+ 5	+ 43	+ 44	– 43	– 14	+ 58

Source:
MORI (*Daily Express*).
FW: 21–6 April 1979.

Table 6.4 *Election Readership by Party Support*

(*n* =)	All (1,025) (%)	Conservative (407) (%)	Labour (379) (%)	Liberal (112) (%)	(Gallup) (%)
Daily Express	16	23	10	15	16
Daily Mail	13	20	9	10	13
Daily Mirror	24	12	38	16	24
Sun	20	17	26	13	23
Daily Star	4	4	3	2	4
Daily Telegraph	8	13	4	8	10
Guardian	2	1	3	7	3

Sources: MORI (*Daily Express*) and Gallup (*Daily Telegraph*).

Table 6.5 *Party Loyalty by Newspaper Readership*

(n=)	1973 (807)	1974 (1,913)	1975 (3,761)	1976 (3,910)	1977 (3,341)	1978 (4,009)	1979 (4,193)
All	(%)	(%)	(%)	(%)	(%)	(%)	(%)
Conservative	28	30	35	38	38	37	35
Labour	37	41	37	35	36	38	38
Labour Lead	+9	+11	+2	-3	-2	+1	+3
Sun readers							
Conservative	22	16	20	25	26	27	25
Labour	55	57	54	49	48	45	50
Labour Lead	+33	+41	+34	+24	+22	+28	+25
Daily Mirror/ Record readers							
Conservative	17	19	23	21	25	22	20
Labour	59	54	53	51	51	56	57
Labour Lead	+42	+35	+30	+30	+26	+34	+37
Daily Express readers							
Conservative	45	48	51	54	53	50	51
Labour	30	29	25	24	26	27	23
Labour Lead	-15	-19	-26	-30	-27	-23	-28
Daily Mail readers							
Conservative	45	45	50	59	61	55	54
Labour	24	24	25	19	23	23	21
Labour Lead	-21	-21	-25	-40	-38	-32	-33
Daily Telegraph readers							
Conservative	61	52	64	64	71	71	61
Labour	15	15	10	10	11	13	14
Labour Lead	-46	-37	-54	-54	-60	-58	-47

Source:
MORI.
FW: October–November annually.

Table 6.6   *Daily Newspaper Readership by Political Affiliation*

	All	Daily Express	Daily Mail	Daily Mirror	Sun	Daily Star	Daily Telegraph
(Readership)	(100%)	(15%)	(11%)	(24%)	(25%)	(5%)	(8%)
	(%)	(%)	(%)	(%)	(%)	(%)	(%)
Conservative	35	51	54	20	25	21	61
Labour	38	23	21	57	50	61	14
Liberal	10	10	12	7	8	8	12
Labour Lead	+3	−28	−33	+37	+25	+40	−47
(n=)	(4,193)	(629)	(461)	(1,006)	(1,048)	(210)	(335)

Source:
MORI.
FW: October–November 1979.

During the 1979 election campaign itself, MORI also sought to identify how clearly each newspaper's support (as opposed to bias) was identified by its readers. The results were as in Table 6.7.

Table 6.7   *Perceived Party Support of Own Newspaper*

Readers of:	Conservative	Labour	Liberal	None	Don't know
	(%)	(%)	(%)	(%)	(%)
Daily Mail	80	4	2	2	12
Daily Express	82	3	1	1	14
Sun	33	33	1	9	25
Daily Mirror	8	75	1	3	15
Daily Telegraph	92	0	0	4	4

Source:
MORI (*Daily Express*).
FW: 26 April 1979.

In this case there is no question of the answers being distorted by attitudes towards the press in general: each member of the sample was asked about the stance of each newspaper – and the answers shown record the responses of each newspaper's own readers. It seems that small, but measurable, minorities of *Mail, Express* and *Mirror* readers do really believe their paper holds a view opposite to that prominently displayed on the leader, and more than occasionally, news pages. In the case of the *Mirror* the minority amounts to about half a million people. On the other hand, nearly all *Telegraph* readers have got the message; none were labouring under the delusion that their regular paper preferred a Callaghan government.

In the case of the *Sun* the three-way split between Labour, Conservative and none/don't know reflects something of the fluctuations of the newspaper itself. In 1970 shortly after Rupert Murdoch bought it from the Mirror Group, the *Sun* backed Labour after a fashion: 'The *Sun*'s growing army of readers is entitled to know which side their newspaper is on', it announced when the election was called. Answer: 'The *Sun* is on *your* side.' In February 1974, after proclaiming itself as 'the paper in no party's pocket', it gave somewhat hesitant support to the Conservatives. In October 1974 it plumped for an all-party coalition. In May 1979 there was no hesitancy; the *Sun*'s message to its readers was unequivocal – 'Vote Tory' was the message the day the election was called. 'Vote Tory' was the message on election day.

Two years earlier, in 1977, the *Sun* was generally seen as a Labour-biased paper, despite not having backed Labour in a general election for seven years. This is seen from an earlier MORI survey for the *Daily Express*. The question technique was the semantic differential, asking respondents first to rate an 'ideal' newspaper on a seven-point Tory–Labour scale, and then their own paper on the same scale.

Table 6.8   *'Ideal' vs 'Actual' Political Bias*

	Own newspaper			'Ideal' newspaper		
	Pro-Conservative	Neither	Pro-Labour	Pro-Conservative	Neither	Pro-Labour
	(%)	(%)	(%)	(%)	(%)	(%)
All tabloid readers	25	33	38	27	51	21
Readers of:						
Daily Express	55	22	5	36	48	10
Daily Mail	60	34	5	46	50	4
Daily Mirror	10	26	62	19	50	31
Sun	7	45	48	19	53	29
Conservative identifiers	47	31	19	59	36	3
Labour identifiers	9	32	57	4	48	48

Source:
MORI.

A majority of Conservative supporters (59 per cent) want their newspaper to reflect Tory views, while Labour supporters are split equally between a desire for unbiased coverage (48 per cent) and partisan support (48 per cent) (Table 6.8). A third of Tory partisans say they want a strongly Tory paper (they don't think they get it) and 28 per cent of Labour supporters want a strongly Labour one; Labour's most ardent supporters feel themselves reasonably well served on this score.

More *Daily Mail* readers want the *Mail* to be Tory (46 per cent) than *Daily Express* readers the *Express* (36 per cent). Half the readers of each paper (50 per cent and 48 per cent, respectively) want it to be unbiased; only 22 per cent of *Express* readers think it to be so; a third (34 per cent) of *Mail* readers consider it unbiased. One reader in twenty of each paper, possibly reflecting the far right, think the *Express* and *Mail* to be too Labour for their taste (Table 6.8). Furthest out of touch with their readers at that time were the *Daily Express* (too Tory) and *Daily Mirror* (too Labour).

How much does the performance of the press – actual or perceived – matter, given that one of the clichés of our times is that elections are mainly television events? According to MORI's *Sunday Times* panel, it matters a fair amount. MORI asked whether the panel found each of the media useful or not useful in following the election campaign (Table 6.9). Although overall considerably fewer people consider

Table 6.9   *Media Usefulness*

Q. 'How useful do you feel (newspapers/radio/TV) has been in keeping you in touch with what has been happening in the election campaign so far?'

	Useful (%)	Not Useful (%)	Don't know (%)
Television:			
All	75	17	8
Radio:			
All	37	26	36
Newspapers:			
All	53	32	16
Readers of:			
Daily Mail	73	25	2
Daily Express	70	27	3
Daily Mirror	60	28	12
Sun	59	33	8

Source:
MORI.

newspapers useful than thought television useful, for readers of the *Mail* and *Express* their paper was almost as important as the box.

This finding is confirmed by the answers to another question – how much time did members of the panel spend each day following the election in the media? (See Table 6.10).

Table 6.10 *Time Spent Reading/Listening/Viewing*

Q. 'Roughly how much time each day have you spent reading/listening to radio coverage/watching TV coverage of the election?'

	More than 30 min (%)	10–30 min (%)	Less than 10 min (%)	None (%)
On TV	38	32	19	11
On radio	16	15	17	50
In *Daily Express*	36	29	29	6
In *Daily Mail*	27	43	26	5
In *Daily Mirror*	29	27	29	15
In the *Sun*	28	29	30	13

Source: MORI.

Table 6.11 *Media Usefulness*

	Very/Fairly Useful		
	Newspapers (%)	Radio (%)	TV (%)
All	53	37	75
Men	55	37	75
Women	50	38	76
Aged 18–34	49	29	76
Aged 35–54	55	40	73
Aged 55 +	52	42	77
ABC1	57	46	77
C2	54	32	77
DE	47	33	72

Source: MORI, *Sunday Times* Panel, 17–19 April 1979.

Even a clear majority of *Sun* readers claimed to have spent at least ten minutes a day following the election in their paper. Since MORI did not ask the panel to measure their use of time with stopwatches, these figures should be regarded as *perceptions* of how people spent their time. But that, in its way, is as important as the actual time spent – for whatever time people actually spent following the election on the different media, they *believed* they spent almost as much time following it in the press as on TV. And that belief confirms the idea that newspapers are almost as important as television in helping the public follow a general election campaign.

One of the myths of political communications is that radio is a young people's medium. Not for political communication it isn't. In fact, Table 6.11 shows that radio was seen as useful mostly to older, ABC1, respondents.

But what of the role of local newspapers whose impact, according to Labour MPs' and candidates' grass-roots opinions, is a powerful influence on the opinion and attitudes of electors in their districts? (There may be a tendency, we believe, for their view to be coloured by the ease with which they themselves achieve exposure.) Evidence is scant. What have been measured are the second-hand opinions in the last election from MORI's post-election postal survey of Labour candidates (488 of the 622 candidates responding – 78 per cent). While current wisdom would suggest that local papers are overwhelmingly Tory in their views, Labour candidates don't think so. In fact, according to the survey, 70 per cent said their local newspaper made no voting recommendation, a quarter (26 per cent) did urge their readers to vote Tory and the other 5 per cent or so split between Labour, Liberal and nationalists.

Finally, we thought it would be instructive to compare the public's readership with such 'opinion leader' or 'elite' groups as members of Parliament, trade union leaders and TUC conference delegates and the press. The first thing that strikes us about this is how 'up-market' MPs' readership is compared to the electorate – very few MPs read the popular Sundays – but this is perhaps unsurprising. What is perhaps more surprising is how little trade union leaders read the papers their members read (only 11 per cent read the *Sun* and 19 per cent the *Daily Mirror*, compared to a third who read the *Daily Telegraph*, 41 per cent the *Financial Times* and 72 per cent the *Guardian*) (Table 6.12).

Summary

- Nearly a quarter of the public perceive British newspapers generally as biased towards the Tories; more, over a third, believe the press is unbiased.
- Twice as many people consider the BBC to be biased Tory (9 per cent) as Labour (4 per cent), but most people (70 per cent) consider BBC TV unbiased.

Table 6.12   *Newspaper Readership*

(n =)	(1) General Public (4,221) (%)	(2) MPs (100) (%)	(3) Trade Union General Secretaries (81) (%)	(3) TUC Conference Delegates (91) (%)	(4) Industrial and Labour Journalists (21) (%)
Daily Newspapers:					
Daily Express	15	19	19	16	67
Daily Mail	11	37	11	19	67
Daily Mirror	24	23	19	41	77
Sun	25	15	11	12	48
Daily Star	5	n.a.	5	4	29
Daily Telegraph	8	54	35	23	72
The Times	n.a.	76	n.a.	n.a.	95
Guardian	1	48	72	64	81
Financial Times	1	45	41	16	100
Morning Star	—	n.a.	26	27	43
Evening Standard	n.a.	50	26	12	67
Evening News	n.a.	29	12	8	57
Sunday Newspapers:					
News of the World	24	8	11	15	14
Sunday Mirror	22	7	16	30	24
Sunday People	21	5	19	20	14
Sunday Express	17	53	16	19	33
Sunday Telegraph	7	47	23	21	77
Observer	7	58	73	54	86
Sunday Times	n.a.	80	n.a.	n.a.	95

Source:
MORI:
(1) October–November 1979;
(2) May–June 1978;
(3) Autumn 1979;
(4) January–February 1979.

- ITV and radio are thought unbiased by most.
- Two-thirds of *Daily Express* and *Daily Mail* readers were Tories in May 1979; nearly two-thirds of *Daily Mirror* readers were Labour as were just over half of *Sun* readers.
- Nearly half (43 per cent) of all Tories read either the *Daily Express*, or *Daily Mail*; over 60 per cent of Labour supporters read either the *Daily Mirror*, or *Sun*.
- One person in five doesn't read any daily newspaper.
- The most Labour paper readership is the *Daily Star*; the most Tory is the *Daily Telegraph*.

- At the time of the last election four out of five *Mail* and *Express* readers had got the electoral message – vote Tory – as did nearly all *Telegraph* readers.
- Three-quarters of *Mirror* readers knew their paper wanted Labour returned to office.
- The *Sun*, despite a clear 'vote Tory' line, had a nearly perfect split – one-third Tory, one-third Labour and one-third don't know.
- Most readers want an unbiased newspaper; about a third think they get it.
- Television is thought the most useful election-coverage medium.
- Radio has not, to date, realised its potential, but is most used by older, middle-class electors.

Note: Chapter 6

Peter Kellner was a political writer for the *Sunday Times*, and is now Political Editor of the *New Statesman*; Robert Worcester is Managing Director of Market & Opinion Research International (MORI) and was Polling Adviser to the Labour Party in the 1970, 1974 and 1979 general elections.

7
Television News Coverage of the 1979 General Election

MARTIN HARRISON

The 1979 campaign was the seventh to be reported by television, twenty-one years after Granada's pioneering *essai* at Rochdale. Time enough for politicians, journalists and viewers to take the measure of a new medium, and for 1979 coverage to be seen in a context of relatively settled traditions, routines and rituals. We are concerned here with determining what the election was 'about', as seen through the principal TV news programmes, and with assessing critically the way in which the campaign was handled.

But what *is* election news? As it happens, television normally signals its 'election coverage' quite unequivocally by packaging it distinctively with its own presenters, sets and logos, by direct verbal cues, or by locating it visually amid party promotional material.[1] To follow these various cues of course entails acceptance of the broadcasters' perception of what was 'election' and what was not, and that could at times beg quite important questions, whether one holds that in some sense all reporting is ideological and may thus have electoral implications, or whether one simply looks back to folk memories of the impact on Labour's fortunes of England's World Cup performance. However, in practice, most stories with direct political implications are rapidly absorbed into the campaign exchanges – as the employment and inflation figures were in 1979. A few stories hovered around the margin. The BL and *The Times* disputes were held as routine industrial stories. While the Southall riot attracted a salvo of comment from party leaders within the election coverage, the initial clashes and a subsequent series of incidents over National Front election meetings were almost always kept determinedly separate from the election package. All these were reasonable editorial decisions, yet arguably different editorial and composition criteria might have operated. While it is convenient here to work within the broadcasters' definitions of election news, boundary problems like these must be recognised.

Neither channel was prepared in 1979 to make the quantum leap into the major news-and-analysis operation that was hurriedly mounted and as hurriedly deemed a failure in February 1974. Scheduling and audience considerations held the early evening bulletins at their normal length. The *Nine O'Clock News* stretched from its normal weeknight 23 + minutes to 28–30 minutes, and *News at Ten* from around 25 minutes to 33–5 minutes.[2] The BBC's more modest endeavours must be seen in relation to further coverage in *Nationwide, Campaign '79* and *Hustings*, whereas the news bulletins were the only evening programmes networked on the ITV side. So, while both the early evening news were essentially restricted to spot reports, ITN's larger news hole allowed a wider but possibly less digestible range of reports, surveys and backgrounders. With few big non-election stories to compete, campaign news as usual took a steadily mounting share of the expanded programmes as polling day approached.

Table 7.1 *Election Coverage in Early Evening Bulletins*

	5–11 April (min)	12–18 April (min)	19–25 April (min)	26 April –2 May (min)	Total (min)
BBC	19	25	34	34	111
ITN	27	28	33	40	128

Table 7.2 *Election Coverage in Main Evening News*

	29 March –4 April (min) (%)		5–11 April (min) (%)		12–18 April (min) (%)		19–26 April (min) (%)		26 April –2 May (min) (%)		Total (min) (%)	
BBC	15	9·9	51	32·9	62	42·2	87	47·9	91	50·7	306	37·6
ITN	25	16·1	67	48·4	80	52·7	112	56·4	131	64·1	414	49·0

Figure 7.1 shows in greater detail the leisurely take-off, then the steady rise broken by weekend troughs. This by now traditional pattern may, in fact, say as much about the nature of TV news as about the campaign. Though the parties generated little copy while preparing for battle, they were, apart from an Easter lull, active enough from around 6 April to have sustained greater coverage. The traditional rise to an eve-of-poll peak really owes more to an editorial feeling for dramatic shape than to the 'real' nature of the campaign.

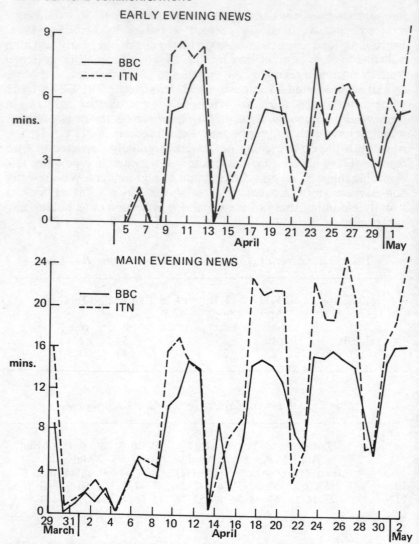

Figure 7.1 Daily flow of election coverage.

Again, though Sunday does still mark a relative lull, the invariable weekend dip reflects overtime costs and the tradition of shorter and lighter bulletins rather than inactivity among the politicians. To a considerable degree the 'shape' of television news flow is a reflection of TV's own structures and routines.

The similarity in the two networks' handling of the election held true at more significant levels. Though there were many differences between them, these were differences within a broadly common system of values and understandings about the nature and importance of the election. Styles of coverage were also strikingly similar; but for a familiar face or tell-tale logo, a casual channel-switcher would often have experienced considerable difficulty in knowing which channel he was watching. Invariably he would have found reinforcement rather than dissonance.

Thus, as Table 7.3 shows, as reported by television this was overwhelmingly a domestic election. For the four weeks 5 April–2 May 1979, the placing of election news was as shown in the table.[3] Major

Table 7.3

	Early		Main	
	BBC	ITN	BBC	ITN
Lead	4	5	9	8
2nd	6	9	6	7
3rd	7	5	5	7
4th	4	3	5	3
5th or lower	7	6	3	3

running stories during the period included the Uganda fighting, teachers' pay, the BL and *The Times* disputes and the Rhodesian elections. Short-run stories included the murder of Airey Neave, the Bhutto execution, the Strasbourg Court ruling on the *Sunday Times* thalidomide article, an IRA trial, a number of attacks in Northern Ireland and several accidents and natural disasters.

More specifically, what the 1979 election was really about, as seen through TV news, was the domestic economy – a cluster of interrelated themes which took up about half the total policy coverage of all four programmes considered here. Early and late, inflation and industrial relations were the leading issues; taxation and employment were dealt with more sketchily in the early bulletins. Only two forthright defences of the benefits of public expenditure were reported over the entire campaign, one from Mr Callaghan and the other from Mr Wilson. Both networks tried to probe the parties' reticence, but with little success. In the light of subsequent events this underweighting of public expenditure, for whatever reason, seems the oddest feature of the news coverage – and a point worth considering in any discussion of 'mandates'.

One could scarcely criticise the dominant play given to 'the

Table 7.4 *Election Coverage in Evening Bulletins*

| | Early Bulletin | | | | Main Bulletin | | | |
| | BBC | | ITV | | BBC | | ITV | |
	(sec)	(%)	(sec)	(%)	(sec)	(%)	(sec)	(%)
Policy Coverage								
Rhodesia	120	1·8	109	1·4	32	0·2	40	0·2
Foreign/Defence	15	0·2	5	–	10	–	71	0·3
EEC	55	0·8	221	2·9	469	2·6	488	2·0
Northern Ireland	115	1·7	100	1·3	530	2·9	310	1·3
Law and Order	218	3·2	65	0·8	227	1·2	857	3·4
Electoral/ Government System	94	1·4	39	0·5	526	2·9	767	3·1
Education	60	0·8	90	1·2	31	0·2	30	0·1
Housing	45	0·6	69	0·9	54	0·3	125	0·5
Social Services	10	0·1	103	1·3	164	0·9	129	0·6
Immigration/ Southall	327	4·9	223	2·9	358	1·9	323	1·3
Environment	88	1·3	80	1·0	88	0·4	308	1·3
Public Expenditure	43	0·6	29	0·4	348	1·8	457	1·8
Taxation	105	1·6	282	3·7	1,143	6·2	803	3·2
Wages and Prices	719	10·7	514	6·7	1,394	7·6	1,424	5·8
Employment	204	2·9	226	2·9	503	2·7	1,444	5·8
Industrial Relations	537	8·0	690	9·0	1,672	9·1	2,616	10·5
(De)nationalisation	24	0·3	21	0·3	43	0·2	104	0·4
Other Economic	284	4·2	255	3·3	635	3·5	847	3·4
General Praise and Blame	449	6·7	411	5·4	1,037	5·6	1,047	4·2
Unclassified	715	10·6	597	7·7	1,436	7·9	1,681	6·8
Total Policy	4,227	62·4	4,129	53·4	10,700	58·1	13,871	55·8
Other Coverage	(sec)	(%)	(sec)	(%)	(sec)	(%)	(sec)	(%)
Polls and Party Prospects	444	6·6	332	4·3	1,839	10·0	2,022	8·1
Politicians' Travels	1,390	20·7	2,714	35·3	2,610	14·2	3,985	16·0
Election Procedure	23	0·3	82	1·1	539	2·9	479	1·9
Campaign Incidents	294	4·4	321	4·2	1,153	6·3	1,229	4·9
Local Regional Surveys	77	1·1	–	–	767	4·2	2,751	11·1
Commentary	90	1·3	–	–	488	2·7	337	1·4
Miscellaneous	173	2·6	142	1·8	257	1·5	192	0·8
Total Other	2,491	37·0	3,591	46·7	7,663	41·8	10,995	44·2
Total	6,718	99·4	7,720	100·1	18,363	99·9	24,866	100·0

economy', particularly the importance attached to inflation and employment. What was lacking was any volume of coverage of the future of the public sector, energy policy, the implications of new technologies or a strategy for reversing the erosion of our industrial base – whether by Mr Benn's approach or Sir Keith Joseph's. Though there were traces of all of these, whether because the parties were saying little or they were under-reported, treatment was scattered and brief.

One need not either take a monetarist view of the economy, or endorse the *Bad News* critique of industrial reporting, to feel that the outcome was a blinkered and skewed treatment of both industrial relations and the power of major economic interests as elements in Britain's economic dilemma. To be sure, television was mostly just doing its job of reporting 'what the politicians were saying', yet the particularly heavy play these themes received owed as much to the editorial 'gate-keepers' as to the parties. The fact that industrial relations stories were relatively less prominent in both the early bulletins, and in BBC coverage compared with ITN's, underlines this. In this area news coverage amplified rather than merely reflected what the politicians did. Without setting the agenda of election issues, television clearly took a role in ranking them.

However the largest single element in election news was the comings and goings of the politicians. From the second week in April every bulletin carried its quota of tour reports. The pattern had been set as far back as 1970. What was fresh in 1979 was the extent to which they dominated the early news particularly and the skill with which the Conservatives set up events calculated to touch a whole series of desired chords.

At times it was hard to recall that a contentious election was under way. Apart from the occasional light-hearted moment, like the appearance of Paddington Bear in one of Michael Cole's reports, the BBC's coverage of these tours was resolutely upbeat, incurious and respectful. If ITN coverage also seemed at times to originate from courtiers rather than reporters, there was also a recurrent lightness, which could verge on condescension or irreverence, as in Anthony Carthew's report that 'there was a walkabout – which meant that Mr Callaghan saw a lot of policemen, and a lot of policemen saw Mr Callaghan'. And here was how Michael Brunson reported the notorious calf episode:

Early today Willersham Farm, near Ipswich, was invaded by one Tory leader, eighty journalists and fifty followers-on, and left the locals speechless. There was a serious reason for the visit . . . but Mrs Thatcher's aides also beamed at the thought of all the pictures this visit would produce . . . [Close-up of Mrs Thatcher surrounded by a babble of cameramen while murmuring endearments to the calf.] And there was a very unusual little news conference. The first, perhaps, ever given by a senior British politician while sitting in a field stroking a 12-hour-old calf. [Long-shot of leader submerged by media men.]

As the campaign went on reports on both channels were sprinkled with words like 'razzamatazz' and 'media circus' or equally pointed long-shots of scrimmages. At times reporters came as close to 'knocking' their assignments publicly as one is ever likely to find. For ITN, Michael Brunson commented strongly on the risk to life and limb during Mrs Thatcher's visit to a Paddington old people's home, and Anthony Carthew described Mr Callaghan's visit to a supermarket in equally critical terms.

Elections are exercises in advocacy, not a confessional. Whether their leaders or policies are on display, parties will naturally contrive to appear advantageously. But where a Labour speech on taxation could be challenged by a Conservative one, tested in a news conference question, or analysed in a briefing report, such rounded coverage on matters of personality is all but impossible. Parties may criticise opponents politically but rarely personally, while for TV journalists themselves to challenge directly the version of a leader's personality on public display, is all but unthinkable. In short, where personal qualities are concerned, there is really no possibility of balanced reporting. That is really no place for self-respecting journalists to be.

The 'spread' of coverage between individuals and parties can be discussed more briefly. As early as 1964 campaign news was concentrating heavily on a few party leaders, while the 1966 election was particularly 'presidential' in presentation.[4] In 1979 Mr Callaghan took 60 per cent of BBC1's coverage of Labour politicians and 67 per cent of ITV's, while Mrs Thatcher took 63 per cent and 61 per cent, respectively, and Mr Steel 69 per cent and 80 per cent. The concentration on the three leaders was higher than in either of the 1974 campaigns, though the number of politicians featuring in radio and TV news (eighty-five) was the largest since coverage began.[5]

Modern parties want to 'sell' their leaders as well as (or instead of) their policies. In 1979 it was the Conservatives who had special political and tactical reasons for plugging coverage of Mrs Thatcher. Always ready to personalise, and worried lest some newsworthy incident affecting a party leader should occur away from their cameras, editors now invariably commit a sizeable slice of their resources to following the leaders, thereby leaving other stories by the wayside and putting themselves under a measure of pressure to get value for money by running some of the footage. And indeed, on any analysis, it would be a curious form of reporting which failed to deal prominently with the parties' chief spokesmen and standard bearers.

Yet it is questionable whether 'reality' or 'news value' decreed that Mr Callaghan (60 per cent of Labour time) should be more than six times as favoured as Mrs Williams on BBC1, or Mr Healey on ITN (both with 9 per cent), or that Mrs Thatcher (61 per cent of Conservative time) should so outdistance her nearest colleague (Mr Prior, with 6 per cent on BBC1 and 7 per cent on ITN).[6] A closer look at the flow of coverage shows just how far this outcome reflected day-to-day editorial judgements rather than the categorical imperative of events. To take an admittedly crude yardstick, if for each day coverage had been limited to the level of whichever channel gave less time on that day, then over the campaign as a whole Mr Callaghan would have had 27 per cent less exposure than he actually received in BBC early news and Mrs Thatcher 29 per cent less. By comparison with BBC main news output the reductions would have been 15 per cent and 17 per cent, respectively. (In relation to ITN's more copious coverage the differences would be more striking still: minimum treatment of the two leaders would have been 43 per cent and 33 per cent lower than actual exposure in the early news, and 31 per cent and 32 per cent, respectively, for the main news.)

Fragile and artificial though the exercise is, it nevertheless emphasises the leeway even within conventional professional assessments of news values, for varying the mix of attention to politicians. Within the given volume of news there was scope for featuring second-rank figures rather more often, or giving them a longer run when they did appear. Current news conventions make an assessment of the team almost impossible. Second-rankers are not so newsworthy, but they may be better informed about their specialist field – quite apart from the possibility that a more varied selection of faces might be of greater audience interest than the eternal Jim and Maggie show.

It would be churlish not to recognise the achievement of TV election news in an impossible task. It is called on to give a rapid, comprehensive and fair report for a mass audience of an exceptionally complex happening, with limited resources and an uneasy awareness, in 1979, of the hypersensitivity of politicians who hold the key to higher licence revenues and the future of broadcasting. And all this in the knowledge that its coverage may be necessary but is not greatly loved. Somehow there emerges a highly professional flow of news which over the years has done much to curtail the partisan excesses of a committed press, and to persuade the parties to talk to rather than past one another.

Yet the conventions and balances of coverage call for further reflection. Election news can range from the outright 'producerist' to the totally passive. In 1979 the balance was well towards passivity. Partly this was a consequence of the inherent passivity of tour coverage. But – without usurping the parties' role – there was scope for tougher questions in the news conferences or from reporters on the campaign trail, where hackneyed questions were rolled out again and again. There was room for more policy briefing reports of the kind both channels featured modestly.

Again, while the 1979 coverage avoided the 'issue-a-day' approach of certain past campaigns, it tended to plug a handful of fashionable issues too hard, while failing to pick up important if less prominent issues. The 'herd instinct' among journalists is well enough established to be worth guarding against. Similarly with individuals, the conventions have tilted towards an over-concentration on a handful of politicians. This gives cheaper and easier coverage, and seems to find acceptance with the parties. But it does not necessarily reflect the character either of the election, or of British government. Nor is it particularly interesting.

These are all in effect arguments for more active, enterprising and imaginative election reporting, and for a wider spread of coverage of issues and individuals, in line roughly with current commitments in time and resources. While election reporting which is true to the event is bound to be heavily repetitive because the essence of electioneering is to hammer home just a few basic themes, it does not have to be repetitive in the *way* 1979 was repetitive. We have tried to show that even within the networks' conventional values and routines – which some might be disposed to challenge more radically – there was considerable scope for a different mix and balance of coverage than was actually presented. Although elections are invariably said to be covered on 'news value', election news values are in many respects radically different from those applying in 'peace time'. It is doubtful whether more than 10 per cent of election coverage would have been carried had it occurred outside the election period. Despite the special legal limitations on election reporting and the need to hold the major parties in approximate stopwatch balance, the very suspension of some of the normal yardsticks offers journalists a measure of flexibility and not simply constraints.

Election news in 1979 often gave the impression of being prepared with one eye on the parties and one eye on the editors, leaving no eye for the viewers. We have already noted that election coverage is not particularly popular with its audience. Partly this can be a matter of viewers becoming restive at being reminded of unpleasant problems or reacting adversely to the parties' antics – though to some extent those antics reflect politicians' assessments of what the news rooms will 'buy'. But sometimes the public may well have been reacting to the messenger rather than the message. Though stitched together with consummate professionalism, the nightly news packages at times seemed tailor-made to demonstrate the dangers of a 'bias against understanding'.[7] Coping with the multiple verbal and visual changes of direction was highly demanding – sometimes too demanding, with upwards of twenty stories in as many minutes, some of them split into several segments. At times ITN packed points from six speeches into 50 seconds. The median length of speech extracts on the *Nine O'Clock News* was about 45 seconds, and on *News at Ten*, 25 seconds. Quite apart from the limits to democratic dialogue implicit in such figures, this can be very hard to follow. Reports of the party manifestos were also prone to become breathless catalogues of promises. In looking to the next campaign television needs to think in terms of not only being more active and varied, but of working towards forms of presentation which might communicate their efforts to the voters more successfully. Ultimately, after all, it is *their* election. To the extent that television forgets this its professionalism and its public-spirited commitment of resources are largely deployed in vain.

Notes: Chapter 7

Martin Harrison is Professor of Politics at the University of Keele.

1 Where only one channel handled an item as election news, the relevant material was credited to campaign coverage in both cases. A few stories on local elections were excluded, though presented in the election sequences. These exceptions do not materially affect results.
2 Calculations exclude opening and closing sequences, headlines and the *News at Ten* break sequence.
3 All calculations relate to early evening bulletins, 5 April–2 May 1979, and main news programmes, 29 March–2 May.
4 D. E. Butler and A. King, *British General Election of 1966* (London: Macmillan, 1966), p. 130.
5 D. E. Butler and D. Kavanagh, *British General Election of 1979* (London: Macmillan, 1980), p. 209. The calculations refer to a slightly different period and sample of bulletins but hold broadly true for the ground we are covering here.
6 Butler and Kavanagh, op. cit., p. 209.
7 J. But and P. Jay, 'The radical changes needed to remedy TV's bias against understanding', *The Times* (1 October 1975).

8

The *Granada 500*: a Continuing Experiment in TV General Election Coverage

BOB SELF

Most of the major questions relating to television election coverage had been largely settled before the May 1979 general election and Granada Television had been in the forefront of these innovations.[1] During the 1970s, for instance, *The Granada 500* played a major role in the development of political broadcasting. First screened during the February 1974 campaign, the *Granada 500* had been designed to change the emphasis of television election coverage from the reporting of platform rhetoric to substantive discussion of issues which the electorate considered to be important. In particular, this meant bringing politicians in contact with large television audiences: a proposal which had been continuously and vigorously resisted by the Parliamentary Broadcasting Committee until October 1974.

The objective of this paper is to review the *Granada 500* programmes of the 1979 campaign. More specifically, the paper attempts to demonstrate that in realising the objectives of its architects the *Granada 500* not only provided an important channel of political communication during the 1979 general election to the Granada Television region, but also had a marked effect upon those members of the Bolton East electorate who became the *Granada 500* and whose participation in the series directly exposed them to an unusually high level of political information.

Background

The basic format of the *Granada 500* series during the 1979 campaign was similar to that used successfully in the two 1974 elections.[2] Perhaps the most obvious difference was that the venue for the programmes had been moved from the two Preston constituencies to

Bolton East. This was, however, a relatively superficial difference in that Bolton East, like Preston, is situated in the heart of the Granada region and was regarded both demographically and electorally as a microcosm of the country as a whole.[3]

Two days after the election was announced, Market & Opinion Research International (MORI) interviewed an interlocking quota sample of 1,168 Bolton East electors.[4] The purpose of this poll was twofold: to recruit people living in the constituency to participate in the *Granada 500* series and, secondly, to establish a baseline of Bolton East electors who could be re-interviewed later in the campaign, in order to monitor changing opinions within the constituency in general and among *Granada 500* participants in particular. Having established a panel baseline during 31 March–3 April, MORI recalled the panel on 26–28 April and conducted a post-election postal recall over 5–27 May. The polling exercise was, therefore, a fundamental and integral part of the *Granada 500* experiment.

One immediate value of the polling exercise was to introduce a 'democratic' element into the series by permitting the electors of Bolton East to select the topics for discussion in the eight local programmes. This was achieved by asking respondents at the beginning of the campaign which problems facing the country *should* politicians concentrate on during the election. The frequency of response to this question dictated the choice of subject for discussion and provided a provisional guide for programme scheduling.

The programmes themselves were recorded at the Octagon Theatre, Bolton, shortly before transmission. The programme format was similar to that used successfully in 1974 in which *Granada 500* participants put questions to panels of experts selected to give a balanced view on the particular issue under discussion. The issues covered were, in programme order, the cost of living – prices; the cost of living – wages and taxation; law and order; unemployment; education; pensions and benefits; housing; and industrial relations.

One very important difference from the 1974 series, however, was that the programmes were broadcast at 7.00 p.m. to 7.30 p.m. in 1979 instead of 2.00 p.m. to 2.30 p.m.: a change prompted by the desire to improve the representativeness of the programme participants, who in 1974 had been predominantly housewives and the retired. Where necessary Granada also made arrangements with local employers to release *Granada 500* members from work early, in order to attend the programmes.

The purpose of the eight local programmes had been to inform and de-mystify the issues for the Granada region. For *Granada 500* participants, however, they also served as an introduction to the discipline of television in preparation for the climax of the series when they would be dispatched to London on a special train three days before polling to put their questions to the three party leaders. In the pre-election negotiations Granada's ability to guarantee that the *Granada 500* would be a genuinely representative sample of Bolton East electors already accustomed to the discipline of television had been a critical factor in persuading the party leaders to co-operate in the making of the series.

For some years before 1974, Granada had held the view that television election coverage should be used to permit voters to question those who wished to enter Parliament as their representatives. It was not until the October 1974 campaign, however, that the three party leaders participated in a *World in Action Special*, where they separately faced the questioning of the *Granada 500* sample. This innovation established what has become a new election 'tradition' and ended an era in which politicians regarded large television audiences with at least grave suspicion and frequently with little short of outright hostility.

After the success of the October 1974 experiment, Granada hoped to retain the initiative at the next election by staging a 'Great Debate' in which the party leaders would confront each other. Though the negotiations with the parties over such a debate ultimately proved unsuccessful, David Kemp (a prominent figure in political broadcasting and the producer in charge of the *Granada 500* in 1979) had continued to operate a parallel strategy during these negotiations. He recognised that if it was not possible to stage a 'Great Debate', he would have had to produce an alternative election programme. Three days before the election, a one-hour *World in Action Special* was thus broadcast throughout the independent television network, in which the three party leaders again separately faced the questions of the *Granada 500* members. Although it was not the hoped for 'Great Debate', it proved a fitting climax to the series and arguably produced one of the most surprising poll findings of the whole campaign.

The 'Great Debate'

In terms of the public's perception of personality, Mr Callaghan had always enjoyed a substantial advantage over Mrs Thatcher and by March 1979 it was commonly held that the avuncular image of Mr Callaghan would compare very favourably in live debate with the aloof condescension of Mrs Thatcher. Yet, as Table 8.1 illustrates, the electors of Bolton East believed Mrs Thatcher performed rather better than Mr Steel and considerably better than Mr Callaghan in answering the questions of the *Granada 500* participants.

Table 8.1 *Who Won the 'Great Debate'?*

Q. Which of the three party leaders did you think came across best in the programme?

	Mr Callaghan (%)	Mrs Thatcher (%)	Mr Steel (%)	No Answer (%)
All	19	46	33	2
Men	22	40	37	1
Women	17	50	30	2
Aged 18–24	22	18	57	3
25–34	16	43	40	2
35–54	15	40	42	3
55+	22	58	18	1
Voted on 3 May:				
Conservative	2	75	20	2
Labour	41	20	39	1
Liberal	3	17	76	3

Base:
All who watched/took part in programme.
Source:
MORI (post-election recall, 5–27 May 1979).

Three points about Table 8.1 are perhaps worthy of closer scrutiny. First, although men were generally believed to be less favourably disposed towards Mrs Thatcher than women, there was a relatively small difference in the evaluation of the leaders' performance between sexes. Moreover, if there was a misogynist vote, Mr Steel rather than Mr Callaghan benefited from its existence. Secondly, although Mrs Thatcher's performance rating increased with age and Mr Steel's decreased with age, Mr Callaghan's rating was uniformly dismal among all age groups. Finally, the evidence suggests that partisanship was a far less important factor in evaluating the leaders' performance than might have been expected: a finding which supports the view that the *Granada 500* perceived themselves primarily as representatives of the Bolton East electorate rather than as committed party supporters. Thus, although three-quarters of those who voted either Conservative or Liberal on the 3 May thought their party leader had performed best, only two-fifths of Labour voters could say the same of Mr Callaghan.

Partisanship is even less tenable as an explanation for Mr Callaghan's poor performance rating in the context of MORI's recall survey completed only two days before the programme was filmed.

This survey showed that Mr Callaghan's image profile had improved considerably during the campaign (see below).

In this context, therefore, Mrs Thatcher's superior performance rating in the *World in Action Special* is even more surprising. In the absence of any other evidence the explanation must be largely attributed to the quality of Mrs Thatcher's performance and the contrast between her style and that adopted by Mr Callaghan.

In facing the *Granada 500* the Conservative leader appeared relaxed, candid and quietly confident without giving the impression of condescending complacence. Although allocated the same amount of time as Mr Callaghan, she answered fewer questions but did so in such a way as to lend credence to her assertion that she 'could go on and answer a lot more'.

In contrast to Mrs Thatcher's friendly, relaxed manner, Mr Callaghan arrived at the Greenwood Theatre in a state of considerable anxiety, and just before entering the studio he expressed doubts about participating in the programme at all. Press reports the following morning tended to emphasise the fact that Mr Callaghan faced an audience far less sympathetic and tolerant than that which had greeted Mrs Thatcher a few minutes before.[5] Certainly, one questioner did ask Mr Callaghan to comment on what he described as the government's 'miserable record', but it is difficult to interpret this as evidence of inherent audience bias, first, because Mr Callaghan entered to the warmest welcome of the afternoon and, secondly, because only two days before the MORI recall of the panel had given him a fourteen-point lead over Mrs Thatcher as the better potential Prime Minister. Replying to questions, however, Mr Callaghan appeared nervous and edgy; an impression substantiated by his tendency to reply before questioners had finished speaking. Moreover, he personalised the issues and occasionally made disparaging references to the Conservative leader, a strategy conspicuously avoided by both his rivals. Probably most important in alienating audience support, however, was his frequently aggressive attitude towards his questioners. To a supplementary question on pay from a nurse, for instance, the Prime Minister replied in a hectoring voice: 'What's wrong with that, love? . . . It's no use shaking your head love, these are the facts!' The facts may have been incontrovertible but the manner in which they were expressed was disastrous for Mr Callaghan.

Mrs Thatcher's apparently greater confidence in facing the *Granada 500* programme may be explained, at least in part, by the professionalism of Central Office in preparing for the programme. As one of the Granada team observed, for both Labour and Liberal party managers the *Granada 500* was 'just another date in an already full appointment book': a stark contrast to the Conservatives who spent some time with David Kemp discussing the background to the series, inquiring about the colour of the background, the lighting arrangements, whether the camera would focus on Mrs Thatcher's 'good side' and even the height of her chair. Whatever the explanations, in view of Mrs Thatcher's superior performance rating in the *Granada 500*, had the Conservatives lost the 1979 general election they may have looked back upon their rejection of Labour's challenge to a public debate as one of the great missed opportunities of the campaign.

The Survey

One of Granada's objectives in commissioning MORI to conduct a panel study in Bolton East was to attempt to determine whether abnormal and direct exposure to political stimuli, such as those involved in attending the *Granada 500* programmes, correlated with any change in opinion. The results from the three stages of the panel suggest very strongly that participation in the series did in fact make a considerable impact upon the *Granada 500* members.

In terms of voting intention the panel study showed that in Bolton East Labour won the campaign convincingly. Labour began the campaign in Bolton East considerably behind the Conservatives but drew almost level by the end of the penultimate week. The shift back to Labour then continued during the final week until, by polling day, Labour had regained enough support to retain the seat. A comparison of the expressed voting intentions of *Granada 500* members with non-participants, however, shows that there was a considerable difference in the magnitude of this shift back to Labour.

From Table 8.2 it appears that when first recruited *Granada 500* participants were slightly but not significantly more Conservative-inclined than non-participants. There was however a significant difference in terms of recall of their 1974 voting, with participants more likely than non-participants to recall voting Conservative in October 1974.[6] There would, therefore, appear to have been a greater real bias towards the Conservatives among participants at the beginning of the campaign. By the end of the campaign, however, there had been a nine-point shift to Labour among *Granada 500* participants compared with only a five-point shift to Labour among non-participants.

An interesting difference emerged between participants and non-participants in relation to those who did not express any voting intention at the beginning of the campaign. Among non-participants 40 per cent of those who expressed no voting intention in the baseline

Table 8.2   *Voting Intention and Recall, by Participation in 'Granda 500'*

	Conservative	Labour	Liberal	Labour Lead
Recall of voting in October 1974				
Granada 500 participants	45	48	7	+3
Non-participants	43	54	3	+11
Voting intention – baseline, 1979				
Granada 500 participants	51	41	7	−10
Non-participants	51	43	6	−8
Voting intention – recall I, 1979				
Granada 500 participants	47	46	7	−1
Non-participants	47	44	9	−3

Base: Recall of 1974: all who voted (937).
    Baseline/recall: all expressing voting intention (1,022 and 833, respectively).
Source:
MORI.

survey continued to do so when recalled in late April, with Labour attracting slightly more 'switchers' from this group than the Conservatives (33 per cent and 26 per cent, respectively). Among *Granada 500* participants, however, only 9 per cent were still uncommitted at the end of the campaign, with Labour doing substantially better than the Conservatives in obtaining the support of these 'switchers' (74 per cent and 17 per cent, respectively). These findings suggest that direct exposure to political information may have been a major factor in the greater degree of 'switching' to a definite party preference among *Granada 500* participants than non-participants.

The existence of a 'participation effect' can be more easily demonstrated in relation to changes in respondents' policy preferences during the campaign. When respondents were asked which party was best at handling various key issues, Labour improved its position considerably on unemployment, prices and industrial relations (though less substantially on law and order) between the baseline survey and recall I.

The existence of a 'participation effect' can be further demonstrated by comparing the movements of opinion among *Granada 500* members and non-members. Although Labour improved its rating on both inflation and unemployment among both groups during the campaign, among *Granada 500* participants the improvement was approximately twice as large as it was among non-participants. The available evidence, therefore, suggests that direct exposure to political information produced a marked 'participation effect' among members of the *Granada 500*.

Although the existence of such a 'participation effect' can only be tentatively suggested from the 1979 data, there can be little doubt as to the interest which the *Granada 500* series aroused in Bolton East and the Granada television region generally. The *Granada 500* series was watched by 47–63 per cent of those watching TV in the region at that time: a programme rating which compares favourably with both the preceding programme (*Granada Reports*) and such programmes as the rural soap opera, *Emmerdale Farm*, which followed it on Tuesday and Thursday. Moreover, for the seven programmes where complete data are available, 42–51 per cent of the *Granada 500* members attended each programme and 49–62 per cent watched each programme.

Conclusion

To conclude, therefore, the *Granada 500* has established a new standard in TV election coverage. In polling terms, the Bolton East panel probably represents the most detailed single constituency election study ever conducted. Moreover, the integration of the polling exercise into the programme format points the way forward to a more imaginative and creative use of polling in election broadcasting and away from the safe but dull (and sometimes even incomprehensible) use of bar and pie-chart presentations. In television terms the *Granada 500* has largely fulfilled the aspirations of its proponents by bringing experts and party leaders before a cross section of the electorate to answer the questions the voters consider important. For members of the *Granada 500*, it was an experience which had a definite effect upon their political opinions. For the Granada region, the series succeeded in imparting large quantities of political information in a manner sufficiently entertaining to attract substantial television audiences. By any standard, therefore, the *Granada 500* must be judged to have made a major contribution to the coverage of the 1979 general election and to the development of political broadcasting.

In retrospect it can be argued that the 'Great Debate' was never really an alternative at the last election, nor will it be in the future, while the problem of Liberal over-representation in election broadcasting remains unresolved. While the House of Commons and British politics generally are dominated by the confrontation between the two major parties, television election coverage is obliged to operate as if a three-party system exists. Liberal over-representation, thus, imposes a major constraint upon the possibilities for innovation in election broadcasting as Granada discovered in their pre-election negotiations with the parties. Nevertheless, the 'Great Debate' between the Conservative and Labour leaders would appear to be an inevitable development. Yet in terms of election coverage this need not necessarily represent a step forward. One of the great strengths of the *Granada 500* experiment was its 'popular' element, in which ordinary people questioned experts and politicians about the issues which concerned them. In contrast, the Carter–Ford debates in 1976 were theatrically staged contests, in which a panel of journalists and other 'experts' questioned the candidates while the audience of electors looked on not as participants, but as silent observers. The *Granada 500* experiment has shown that electors are perfectly capable of asking questions which concern *them* as ordinary voters. While the adoption of the American format for Britain's 'Great Debate' would unquestionably be safer for the party leaders, it may also represent a considerable step backwards from the *Granada 500* in terms of election broadcasting. At present it is sometimes all too easy to forget when watching TV campaign coverage that elections are about ordinary voters as well as politicians. The enduring contribution of the *Granada 500* is that the two can be successfully brought together to both entertain, *and* inform.

Notes: Chapter 8

Bob Self is lecturer in politics at the City of London Polytechnic.

I would like to express my sincere gratitude to David Kemp, producer in charge of the *Granada 500* in 1979, without whose unstinting co-operation this paper would not have been written. Any errors which remain are, of course, my own.

1 See *Granada Goes to Rochdale; A First Report on Constituency Television in a General Election* and *Prelude to Westminster?*, reprinted in the series Granada and Political Broadcasting, 1, 2 and 3 (Granada Television, 1974).

2 For February 1974, see *The Granada 500: An Experiment in Collective Discussion of Election Issues*, Granada and Political Broadcasting, 5 (Granada Television, August 1974). For October 1974, see 'Twice 500', *Independent Broadcasting*, November 1974, pp. 20–21.

3 In 1945 Bolton was a double-member constituency, but from the 1950 general election until October 1974 Bolton East had always returned a candidate to Westminster from the party which ultimately formed the government. A record which it failed to retain in May 1979.

4 For the sample and survey design, see MORI, *'The Granada 500' – Polls in the Bolton East Constituency* (Spring 1979), pp. 1–4.

5 See, for example, Richard Ingrams, 'In the stars', *Spectator* (5 May 1979); John Cunningham, 'Battle of the box', *Guardian* (1 May 1979); and 'Cheers, Maggie', *Daily Express* (1 May 1979).

6 And remember that recalled vote tends in the direction of consistency with present vote intention at time of recall. See, for example, H. T. Himmelweit, M. Jaeger and J. Stockdale, 'Memory for past vote: implications of a study of bias in recall', *British*

Journal of Political Science, vol. VIII, no. 3 (1978), pp. 365-75. See also R. J. Benewick, A. H. Birch, J. G. Blumler and A. Ewbank, 'The floating voter and the Liberal view of representation', *Political Studies*, vol. XVII, no. 2 (1969), pp. 177-95.

9

'Prophets and Wildernesses', Press Coverage of Minor Parties: a Study of the Boundaries of the 1979 Campaign

COLIN SEYMOUR-URE AND ADRIAN SMITH

Introduction

This paper estimates the coverage given to minor parties in the national press during the 1979 general election; speculates upon its character and causes; and discusses the light it throws on the boundaries of electoral politics. A more detailed account of some of the main features is given in an Appendix by Adrian Smith (which can be obtained from him directly).

Why bother with minor parties? Are they not by definition a distraction? To that, a general answer is that their treatment by the press might be a reason why they stay minor. In particular, two factors in the 1979 election promised to make them interesting. First, was the possibility, muted somewhat after the devolution referenda, that the period of two-party dominance might be giving way to a period of minority governments or even a realignment of the party system. Secondly, as the time for an election approached, publicity for the National Front became contentious,[1] the Thorpe affair added uncertainty to the Liberal outlook and the fashion for micro-parties seemed unlikely to decline. How would the press cover it all? On a deeper level, finally, an analysis of this topic might illuminate not only the relation of the press and minor parties, but the communication of electoral politics at large. In the course of reporting an election the press may affect the election itself – not just its substance and outcome, but also popular perceptions of what kind of phenomenon 'the election' is. The particular interest of minor parties is that their treatment might provide insights into newspapers' views of the boundaries of the election: who or what could legitimately be excluded from coverage altogether, or not taken seriously, or treated as a threat to the principles of parliamentary government.

What is a minor party? Press treatment in 1979 suggests distinction into four types. One was the geographically confined party – the Northern Irish and the nationalist parties that might affect the formation of a government. Another was the Liberals, the 'third party' – a significant name because it located them in the main arena of party competition. Next were 'extremist parties', a subtle notion, of left or right, but especially left. Last were micro-parties – the independents, 'no-hopers', cranks; a group about which the press tended to be facetious. Pre-eminent in this group was the Ecology Party, with fifty-three candidates. The others could be separated, not always easily, into the intentionally silly, the unintentionally silly and the serious. (The actual Silly Party candidate, in Dover, intended to be serious and aimed to take votes from the National Front.)

The range of minor party candidates is shown in the attached list from the *Guardian* (Table 9.1). The pattern of coverage is in Table 9.2. Generally, and predictably, the Liberals received most – though

Table 9.1   *Minor Parties, 1979 General Election*

'A record number of candidates will be standing in the general election next week. When nominations closed 2,372 had presented themselves for the voters' choice, compared with 2,232 in October 1974, the previous highest figure:

ACMC – Anti-Common Market Conservative; ACMFE – Anti-Common Market Free Enterprise; ACMOAT – Anti-Common Market On Any Terms; ARPSWR – Air, Road, Public Safety, White Resident; APS – Anti-Party System; Anti-Corr – Anti-Corruption; BSEP – British Socialist Empire Party; Brit C – British Candidate; C – Conservative; CACM – Conservative Against the Common Market; CD – Christian Democrat; CFMPB – Campaign for More Prosperous Britain; CFPG – Child and Family Protection Group; CPPS – Committee for Prevention of Police State; CSA – Christian Stop Abortion; CSD – Christian Social Democrat; Chr Party – Christian Party; CPV – Citizen's Protest Vote; Comm – Communist; Comm Marx-L – Communist Party of England, Marxist–Leninist; Comm Ire Marx–L – Communist Party of Ireland, Marxist–Leninist; Comm PE – Communist Party of England; Cornish N – Cornish Nationalist; DLP – Dog-Lovers' Party; DUP – Democratic Unionist Party; DMPSWR – Democratic Monarchist Public Safety White Resident; Dem Lab – Democratic Labour; Derry Lab – Derry Labour and Trade Union Party; ELPF – East London People's Front; ENP – English National Party; Ecology – Ecology Party; Eng Nat – English Nationalist; FDP – Fancy Dress Party; FG – Fine Gael; FP – Fellowship Party; GLF – Gay Liberation Front; GTB – Go To Blazes Party; ICRA – Irish

Civil Rights Association; IDP – Inter-Dependence Party; IIP – Irish Independence Party; IMG – International Marxist Group; INP – Irish National Party; Ind – Independent; Ind Brit Nat – Independent British Nationalist; Ind C – Independent Conservative; Ind Dem – Independent Democratic; Ind Dem Lab – Independent Democratic Labour; Ind Eng Nat – Independent English Nationalist; Ind Lab – Independent Labour; Ind L – Independent Liberal; Ind L Dem – Independent Liberal Democrat; Ind Rep – Independent Republican; Ind Soc – Independent Socialist; IUU – Independent Ulster Unionist; JHC – Jesus and His Cross; KBUP – Keep Britain United Party; L – Liberal; Lab – Labour; Lab AP – Labour Alliance Party; Lab Co-op – Labour Co-operative; Lab and Dem – Labour and Democrat; Lab Integ – Labour Integrationist; Lab and TU – Labour and Trade Union; LCCP – Labour, Conservative Coalition Party; LDL – Liberal Dog Lover; Mod Lab – Moderate Labour; MCP – Middle Class Party; Meb Kernow – Mebyon Kernow; Nat Front – National Party; NI Lab – Northern Ireland Labour; NB – New Britain; OUP – Official Unionist Party; Ox Ecol – Oxford Ecology Movement; PAA – People and Agrarian; PD – Property Development; PP – People's Party; Peo Cand – People's Candidate; Peo Power – People's Power; Protest P – Protest Party; PTC – Providers Through Care; RF – Rhodesian Front; Rad L – Radical Liberal; Rep Clubs – Republican Clubs; Rev Ref – Revolutionary Reform; Roy – Royalist; SBE – Save Birmingham Education; SDLP – Social Democratic and Labour Party; SLAG – Save London Action Group; SNP – Scottish National Party; SL – Severnside Libertarian; SPGB – Socialist Party of Great Britain; Scot Lab – Scottish Labour Party; Soc Credit – Social Credit; Soc Unity – Socialist Unity; Soc Wkrs – Socialist Workers' Party; Soc Dem – Social Democrat; TOI – Troops Out of Ireland; UCP – United Country Party; UDP – United Democratic Party; UKF – United Kingdom Front; ULP – United Labour Party; UP and Eng Nat – United Party and English Nationalist; UPNI – Unionist Party of Northern Ireland; UU – Ulster Unionist; UUU – United Ulster Unionist; VUPP – Vanguard Unionist Progressive Party; VPP – Volunteer Political Party; Wessex Reg – Wessex Regionalist; Workers' Rev – Workers' Revolutionary Party; WRC – Women's Rights Campaign.'

Source:
Guardian (25 April 1979).

obviously it was not all to their liking, and much was about Mr Thorpe. The *Morning Star* naturally gave most space to the Communist Party. The violence at Southall on 23 April and its aftermath, including the death of the ANL member Blair Peach, accounted for the attention to the National Front and Anti-Nazi league. (Difficulties of allocation between the two, and between specifically NF/ANL stories and law and order generally, require these figures to be treated as tentative.) Taken together, coverage for these two parties easily outweighed that for the Liberals in the *Daily Express* and *Daily Mail*.

Beyond this, 'pattern' is altogether too tidy a word to describe the space for minor parties. The quantities are minute: in the *Daily Telegraph* and *Sun* the string of micro-parties appears entirely because of one article about the phenomenon. The Ecology Party pushed up a modest molehill in several papers. Auberon Waugh's Dog-Lovers' Party did so in rather more (and inspired predictable cartoons). 'Serious' parties certainly did not get more attention everywhere than 'silly' ones.

Why Cover Minor Parties at All?

Two considerations broadly determine the answer to this question. Parties won coverage either because of the way they seemed to fit into the election itself, or because they satisfied a criterion of newsworthiness to which the election was secondary. These two factors apply to the major parties in an election as well; but the newsworthiness criterion especially is for them a determinant simply of the shape of the campaign rather than of whether they get reported at all.

FITTING IN TO THE ELECTION

Election campaigns are organised in predictable routines, culminating in the ritual gesture of the cross on the ballot slip. Press coverage follows – indeed, helps to organise – those routines. The more minor parties fit into them, the more likely they are to get coverage. 'Fitting in' means having demonstrable relevance to the routines – publishing a manifesto, qualifying for an election broadcast, featuring in an opinion poll – or else to the major party battle which is the stuff of the election.

The Liberals, clearly, scored well in 1979 on both grounds. Therein lies the significance of the 'third-party' tag. Any party already represented in the Commons is, so to speak, licensed for publicity. Thus, David Steel was invited to publish articles on a par with the major party leaders (for example, the *Sun*, 1 May); the Liberal manifesto was reported in detail and taken up in leading articles; the daily Liberal press conference featured alongside the other parties'. All this led to what Peter Jenkins teasingly called 'Disproportional representation' for the Liberals in the media (*Guardian*, 16 April). It was epitomised in David Steel's 'Battlebus'. For several elections Liberals have had a transportation image. Perhaps it dates from Mr Thorpe's use of hovercraft and helicopter; or, more likely, from the fact that the leader of a serious national party has to travel, and his form of transport is a clue to party resources. Nearly every paper had

Table 9.2 National Daily Newspaper Coverage of Minor Parties, 5 April–3 May 1979

	Daily Express		Daily Mail		Daily Mirror		Daily Star		Daily Telegraph		Financial Times		Guardian		Morning Star		Sun	
	(cm²)	(%)	(cm²)	(%)	(cm²)	(%)	(cm²)	(%)	(cm²)	(%)	(cm²)	(%)	(cm²)	(%)	(cm²)	(%)	(cm²)	(%)
Liberal Party	2,058	30·0	3,599	39·8	1,804	59·0	3,208	63·5	5,926	58·4	6,850	74·6	7,670	51·2	425	2·3	4,328	62·2
Anti-Nazi League	1,395	20·0	2,764	30·6	375	12·3	310	6·1	1,398	13·8	286	3·1	568	3·8	2,057	11·0	399	5·7
National Front	2,302	33·0	1,465	16·2	754	24·6	295	5·8	1,462	14·4	401	4·4	3,312	22·1	3,740	20·1	720	10·3
WRP	44	1·0	224	2·5					130	1·3	47	1·0					137	1·9
Ecology Party	32	–	246	2·7	19	–			230	2·3	26	–	640	4·2	42	–	54	1·0
SNP	257	3·7	133	1·5	5	–	75	1·5	494	4·9	699	7·6	1,111	7·4	400	2·1		
Plaid Cymru	6	–	20	–					80	–	128	1·4	477	3·2	190	1·0		
Communist Party	97	1·4	50	–					102	1·0	188	2·0	20	–	11,691	63·0		
Dog-Lovers' Party	350	5·0	532	5·9	102	3·3	1,046	20·7	180	1·7	123	1·3	888	5·9	16	–	135	1·9
Socialist Workers' Party											50	–					348	5·0
Royalist (J. King)	440	6·3	5	–			119	3·8	9	–								
Silly Party									6	–	9						16	–
Scottish Labour Party									26	–	152	1·6	36	–				
Socialist Unity											50							
Wessex Regional Party									12	–	141	1·5	38	–			72	1·0
Democratic Monarchist Party									20	–	12	–					60	1·0

Independent (Trepanning)	8	–						233	3·3
Ban Old Fogeys Party								308	4·4
United County Party	12	–						152	2·2
Independent Socialist	4	–			48	–			
Moderate Labour Party	12		7	–					
Campaign for More Prosperous Britain	35	–	6	–					
Abstentionist Party	40	–			140	1·0			
Independent Labour Party					14	–			
English National Party									
Cornish Nationalist Party	4	–							
Others	7	–	7	–	4	–			
Total	7,016	9,038	3,059	5,053	10,155	9,182	14,966	18,561	6,962

Notes:
All figures are approximate. Allocation of space between the ANL and NF after the Southall clashes is in some cases difficult and the two groups are best considered in aggregate. Scottish, Welsh and Northern Irish parties were originally excluded from the analysis, which was intended to consider only 'extremist' parties. It has been possible in the end to include only Scottish and Welsh.
The measurement and analysis were carried out by Miss Maxine Dixon and Mrs Riemke Riemersma.

a picture of the Battlebus or David Steel inside it, with stories of its fixtures and particularly those which (characteristically, somehow) did not quite work. Later several papers had features about David Steel on the hustings in it.

The Liberals being the only national third party were the only one to get such national treatment. For all minor parties, including the Scottish and Welsh Nationalists and the Northern Irish, regional and constituency surveys were one of the newspaper routines which provided spasmodic coverage, mainly but not exclusively in the broadsheet papers. The nationalists were of interest because they might impinge on major party fortunes; and hence they cropped up in opinion-poll coverage too.

Another index of importance was the number of candidates a party fielded. Early, if small, notice was given to the National Front, Workers' Revolutionary Party, Communist Party and Ecology Party, for this reason. Moreover, numbers meant election broadcasts – for four of these parties. This fact itself led to publicity: it was the only publicity the Ecology Party got at all in the *Daily Mirror*. The *Daily Telegraph* (21 April) complained that extremist parties could in effect buy air time for the price of fifty lost deposits. The broadcasts themselves then qualified as a routine subject of press coverage. The *Daily Telegraph*'s short leading article on Corin Redgrave's WRP broadcast was the main publicity the party received in that paper (25 April).

Broadcasting was a source of coverage in one other way. The Scottish Nationalists' attempt to ban ITN broadcasts north of the border unless they included fair coverage of the SNP was the lead story on the *Financial Times* election news page (14 April) and attracted attention elsewhere (for instance, the *Guardian*, the *Star*). It was a neat illustration of the way a minor party would be reported when it had major-party implications.

Manifestos, lastly, have always been a hitching-post for party coverage on the campaign trail. Early coverage for the parties just discussed was hooked to their manifestos. These provided the occasion too for publicity about the Dog-Lovers' Party (probably because Mr Thorpe successfully sought to have publication of the manifesto banned), and the Communist Party, Plaid Cymru and the Wessex Regional Party.

GENERAL NEWSWORTHINESS

The second general reason for reporting minor parties was when they did something which satisfied ordinary news values; something exciting, unusual, unexpected, full of action and human interest and preferably involving well-known people. 'Dog bites man' might do for the major parties; for the others, it had to be 'man bites dog'.

The major news story of the election, by these criteria, was the National Front/Anti-Nazi League/police clash in Southall (on which more below). News of the Front hitherto had been only small items based on the considerations just discussed.

The best minor party personality, whose affairs were a *leitmotiv* throughout the election, was Jeremy Thorpe. Much Liberal coverage was actually Thorpe coverage – the postponement of his trial which had been due to start early in the campaign; the avoidance by David Steel of his constituency; his injunction against Auberon Waugh's election manifesto; and his determined candidacy and campaign. Thorpe in the campaign was summed up by John Akass: foreign journalists, he noted, 'regard the British general election as simply another episode in the Thorpe story' (*Sun*, 20 April).

The unusual and the unexpected were also criteria that brought the Liberals coverage. Attacks on the leadership by the Young Liberals Conference at Easter were widely reported. The Liberal candidate in Mr Callaghan's constituency, who decided to withdraw and urged constituents to vote Conservative and get Mr Callaghan out, received enormous publicity. In the *Star* he was given more space to write an article than was Mr Steel himself.

'Unusual' shades into 'odd'. A whole range of independents and micro-parties gained brief mention apparently on grounds of eccentricity. The keynote was struck by the *Guardian*. Announcing its campaign plans on 3 April it promised 'the most comprehensive, the most informed, the most entertaining' coverage. But entertainment may come at the expense of seriousness, and the *Guardian* promised coverage of 'the antics of the no-hoper candidates'. 'Hoper' candidates (Mrs Thatcher and Mr Callaghan, for example) do press conferences and speeches. No-hoper candidates do antics. Of course, Mrs Thatcher might do antics too (there was the matter of her holding the baby calf); but not *only* her antics would be reported. The danger for micro-parties was that they would be presumed unserious and treated as light relief just because they were no-hopers. They were not even a sideshow, for sideshows are at least part of the fair. They were an intrusion, an incongruity and, because odd, funny.

It is difficult, admittedly, not to accept some of the micro-parties on these terms – the candidate whose platform was trepanning; the man who stood in four constituencies and campaigned on a bicycle with a canopy to keep out the rain; the parties with silly names (the Fancy Dress Party, the Go To Blazes Party). The difficulty for the press and its readers was in separating these from the 'serious' ones. Was the Wessex Regional Party candidate who 'frequently dresses entirely in silver leather and also swims nude in the sea at Clovelly' perfectly encapsulated in that description in the *Sun* (18 April)? Or was she the victim of tabloid news values and prose?

Parties quoted on entertainment grounds included a specifically showbiz element. Pop singer Jonathan King, standing as a Royalist, received in the *Daily Express* about six times as much coverage (in the form of an enormous photograph with Barry Humphries, and accompanying text) as the Workers' Revolutionary Party and Ecology Party put together. David (Screaming Lord) Sutch, standing as the Ban Old Fogeys candidate, received in the *Sun* four times the space of the Ecology Party. The Redgraves tended to get as much space for photographs as for descriptions of WRP policy. Most of the *Daily Express* Ecology Party space went to a diary story about their candidate Edward Goldsmith, Sir James Goldsmith's brother. Patrick Moore, Clement Freud, Auberon Waugh and Viscount Weymouth were others who may have owed publicity to being 'personalities', and sometimes got it in diary columns.

The lesson, in short, is that for some parties publicity came despite their political intent not because of it; or else it might not have come at all. Indeed, the more they could appeal to conventional news values, the less they needed all but a nominal political purpose.

What Sort of Coverage Should Minor Parties Get?

Press coverage of the micro-parties was so small that its quantity and character were determined all of a piece. But for the Liberals, the 'extremist' parties and the ecologists, this question needs analysing further.

Relevance to the major party outcome was bound to be a dominating consideration (subject, in the case of the nationalists, to the pattern of national newspapers' readership). It was natural that there should be interest in the minor parties in the opinion polls, in articles about constituencies where they hoped or needed to win, in analyses of the potential for tactical voting. All this, the press faithfully did – and not just the broadsheet papers.

Editorial preferences were bound to have a bearing too. In contrast with October 1974, when the argument for 'a strong Liberal presence' was widely pressed, the national dailies thought 1979 was no time for blurring the result. No paper wanted a hung Parliament. The furthest any went was to say, like the *Financial Times* (11 April), that 'the main defect of the Liberal Manifesto is probably that it comes from the Liberal Party'. But a Liberal *vote*, it was generally agreed, was at best wasted and – if it should result in a hung Parliament – undesirable.

The Liberals might be a third party, but this particular race ought to be between two horses. Voting Liberal was 'nuts' said the *Sun*; and they were 'wet' said the *Mail*.

More than for several elections, therefore, the Liberals lacked leader-column support. But the distinction drawn by the *Financial Times* was important. For on a second criterion by which papers evidently judged the sort of coverage to give – the minor parties' relevance to major campaign issues – the Liberals attracted detailed attention.

This criterion was even more important for the National Front and its relations with the Anti-Nazi League. Coverage of the topic is described in the Appendix (obtainable from Adrian Smith), but the main features need analysing here. The Front was treated until the clash in Southall on 23 April, about three-fifths of the way through the campaign, according to the criteria discussed in the previous section. Most national dailies gave short summaries of its manifesto and only the *Sun* bothered to make any editorial comment. The Anti-Nazi League, not having parliamentary candidates, had had almost no publicity at all, apart from in the *Morning Star*. A clash between the two groups in Leicester on Saturday 21 April attracted little attention, but the violence surrounding the Front's evening meeting in Southall dominated the headlines for three days and spawned other stories throughout the remainder of the campaign. The contrast of 'before-and-after' coverage is shown in Table 9.3.

Table 9.3 *Coverage of National Front/Anti-Nazi League,*
5 April–3 May 1979: Distribution Before and After
Southall Meeting (Reported, 24 April)

	5–23 April		24 April–3 May		Total	
	(cm²)	(%)	(cm²)	(%)	(cm²)	(%)
Daily Express	81	2	3,516	98	3,597	100
Daily Mail	184	4	4,045	96	4,229	100
Daily Mirror	89	8	1,040	92	1,129	100
Daily Star	88	14	517	86	605	100
Daily Telegraph	180	6	2,680	94	2,860	100
Financial Times	101	15	586	85	687	100
Guardian	415	11	3,465	89	3,880	100
Morning Star	2,195	38	3,602	62	5,797	100
Sun	118	11	1,001	89	1,119	100

Note:
Coverage after 24 April included much that had no direct bearing on the election. This has been excluded from the table, though judgement of the relevance of particular items was necessarily subjective.

Southall linked the Front to issues that were already of concern to the major parties and to principles seen by the press as intrinsic to electoral politics. 'Law and order' was a Conservative policy issue, and here were a couple of extremist groups showing what happens when it is flouted. Beyond the immediate coverage, the event led to discussion about the policy options open to governments to deal with such violence; about the legal and moral claim of the Front to organise marches, qualify for TV broadcasts, expect rate-payers to pay the cost of policing demonstrations (a favourite *Daily Mail* theme); and above all, about the role of the police – in general and and, possibly, in the death of the ANL member Blair Peach.

Concern with the police (a familiar, well-defined institution) led the press to closer scrutiny of the less familiar institutions of the Front and the ANL. Were the police 'in the middle' (the view of most papers) or helping one side, the Front (the view of the *Morning Star*)? Were the two organisations polar opposites, a view nicely indicated in the *Daily Express* (25 April) by George Gale's indictment of 'red fascism'? Or was the ANL entirely different from the brutish simplicities of the Front? Leader comment tended to take the 'polar opposites' view; one which was easily reached if the behaviour of the organisations was considered as distinct from their goals.

Concern with the nature of the two organisations, lastly, may have amplified a preoccupation shared particularly by the *Daily Express* and *Daily Mail* with the danger of an 'extremist' take-over of the Labour party. This too is analysed further in the Appendix (obtainable from Adrian Smith directly). Apart from a return to Benn the bogeyman, its chief elements were the left-wing problems of Newham NE, and a list of forty-three leftist members of Parliament issued by the Social Democratic Alliance.

The effect of Southall, then, was to turn the National Front from a simple participant in the campaign into part of one of the issues (law and order); and to link its opponents, similarly, to one of the themes of Conservative press coverage, the infiltration of 'extremists' into the Labour Party ('entryism'). The Workers' Revolutionary Party and the Ecology Party, paired with no opponents, confronting no one on the streets, browsed in their constituencies and were all but ignored by the press.

Minor Parties and the Press in Electoral Politics

Outside the media, there is no 'national campaign'. National leaders campaign locally; local candidates stand for national parties. It is all put together on TV (for whose benefit the daily press conferences developed in 1959) and in the press.

While not single-handedly creating the campaign, the press does therefore impose upon it order and pattern: the press orchestrates it. The result may not coincide with either major party's own strategy – what issues and personalities should be highlighted, whether the campaign should be 'quiet', and so on. There is always the chance of an external event catapulting in (like Southall) and shifting the emphasis. But pattern there undoubtedly is, if only because the newspapers themselves like to discuss the speeches and issues in a methodical way. For minor parties, however, there is no pattern. Coverage is random and bitty since, as has been suggested, it is determined less by the intrinsic merits of the parties themselves than by their relevance to the major parties and what the press thinks are the important issues, and by their appeal to general news values. Deprived, as it were, of a context, the minor parties are thus virtually doomed to feel their coverage is unfair, trivial, or distorted. The Front, for instance, consistently complained – devoting the first of its two broadcasts to the purpose – that the media concentrated on its racial policy to the exclusion of its other platforms. Indeed, this was one of its arguments for a tactic of ostentatious marches.[2]

In imposing 'order' on the election the press is partly concerned to define, rank and evaluate people, events, issues. The particular need with minor parties is to give them an identity, to help readers locate them in the context of what is already familiar about the election (that is, the major parties and leaders, the existing agenda of national politics).

Where minor parties are already familiar, like the Liberals and the nationalists, giving them definition involves confirming the accuracy of the picture – answering, in effect, the question, 'Is this party quite what it seems?'. Hence, perhaps, the interest in the Liberal Battlebus, and the maverick Liberal candidates. For unfamiliar parties, the search for tabs of identity can be difficult: their ideology may make them talk literally a different language, or they may simply lack indices of weight (a problem for the ecologists).

In the use of tabs of identity an increasingly important factor is the existence of a tabloid press. In 1979 only three papers – one of them the *Financial Times* – were broadsheet (leaving aside the small-circulation *Morning Star*). Table 9.4 shows the distribution of minor-party coverage between 'look-at' and 'reading' material. In the extreme case, the *Daily Mail*, three-quarters of Front/ANL coverage was pictures, headlines and cartoons. In the majority of papers the Front/ANL were treated more 'visually' than other minor parties.

The tabloid factor is as much a matter of presentation as of news values. Photographs and graphic design are capable of great subtlety and might win votes more effectively than words. But arguably they have a reductionist effect – over-simplifying, dramatising and sensationalising. A tabloid paper, if so, is intrinsically more likely than a broadsheet to favour blunt, superficial, populist politics – tabloid parties, in fact. The politics of Southall and the National Front seem more suited to tabloid journalism than does the ideology of the WRP. Instead of ideology, the tabloid approach to the WRP ran like this: 'From wide screen kisses to XXXX – it's all part of the scene these days for Vanessa Redgrave, Oscar-winning actress and parliamentary candidate' (*Sunday Mirror*, 22 April). The picture above showed a naked Miss Redgrave in her latest film, *Yanks*. All parties are subject to the tabloid technique, but in the major parties it is, if the pun is forgiven, less stark.

In the process of defining identities in 1979 the concept which particularly deserves scrutiny is 'extremism'. 'Extremism' characterised the National Front (especially after Southall), the ANL, the WRP and 'Trotskyite' elements infiltrating the Labour Party.[3] But 'extremism' in relation to what? A periphery or two poles? In fact the usage had less to do with the situation of a party than with its stance. The essence of 'extremism' lay in its connotations of threat. 'Extremist' parties had policies that were uncompromising, unbridled, closed to argument. They were likely to subordinate means to ends. They claimed to seek power by the democratic process of elections, but their rhetoric suggested that, once power was achieved, those processes would be abandoned. Alternatively, they might manipulate electoral

Table 9.4 *Percentage Distribution of Newspaper Coverage between 'Graphic' and 'Reading' Material, 5 April–3 May 1979: National Front/Anti-Nazi League Compared with Other Minor Parties*

	NF/ANL percentage of Material			Other Minor Parties percentage of Material		
	'Graphic'	'Reading'	Total	'Graphic'	'Reading'	Total
Daily Express	51	49	100	36	64	100
Daily Mail	75	25	100	37	63	100
Daily Mirror	51	49	100	34	66	100
Daily Star	26	74	100	22	78	100
Daily Telegraph	31	69	100	20	80	100
Financial Times	19	81	100	12	88	100
Guardian	24	76	100	20	80	100
Morning Star	39	61	100	32	68	100
Sun	32	68	100	38	62	100

Note:
'Graphic' includes photographs, cartoons and headlines 1cm or more in depth.

politics to mask the achievement of power for ends incompatible with parliamentary politics. In either case, the subordination of means to ends was the antithesis of constitutionalism and parliamentary democracy, and hence a threat to them.

Since certain minor parties were in that sense extreme, they were themselves appropriately characterised in immoderate language, for example:

'Harmful and thoroughly odious rubbish' – *Daily Telegraph* on Front policies (24 April).

'Crackpot economics, Jingoism and odious racialism' – *Sun* on Front manifesto (18 April).

'Python-style lunacy' – *Sun* TV comment on WRP broadcast (26 April).

'Extremists to War on Police' – *Daily Mail* headlines on Southall violence (24 April).

Because 'extremist' parties posed a threat and had serious intentions, they had to be taken seriously. Such, presumably, would be the reply of the *Daily Mail* and *Daily Express* to a charge of over-reaction in their chasing of the hare of Labour Party 'entryism', for example. The press itself offered two counters to extremism. One was simply to ignore it, since it was not open to argument. The *Star* (28 April), hence, advised people to stay away from Front meetings and strike a blow at 'both neo-Nazis and lunatic far Left, who both feed on disruption and breakdown in law and order'. The same result might be achieved indirectly by forbidding the Front to march in the first place, so that there would be nothing to ignore. The press was generally uneasy at such a prospect, though the *Daily Telegraph* (25 April) declared itself against an unrestricted right to march, and the *Daily Mirror* suggested empowering the police to ban Front marches. The second counter offered by the press was to defuse the threat by mockery. The best example was the *Daily Telegraph*'s leading article (25 April) on the WRP broadcast.

'Extremism', then, had as much to do with a party's methods as with its goals. Thus, the Labour Party extremists were objectionable in part at least because they pretended to represent a majority but were in fact only a small minority. Similarly, in a leading article on 'The shifting middle ground' the *Daily Telegraph* argued that Mrs Thatcher's policies did not move her party to the right but simply re-occupied the real 'middle ground' which represented the feelings of the British people and which had been abandoned for a spurious middle ground defined in relation to the leftward tendency of a period of Labour government.

In so far as goals were the reference-point of 'extremism', they were those of the established parties. Any minor party that played by the rules of the parliamentary game and yet had no ideology related to a major party was less likely to be called 'extremist' than 'cranky' or 'lunatic'. The ground for this was that either their members or their policies were, in brief, potty. Yet because they were small and did not seek a short cut to size, they posed no threat. There were elements of this approach even in some of the comments quoted here about the Liberals. The ecologists were especially prone to be approached in this way.

Conclusion

On the evidence of an impression of the 1979 campaign, a minor party will be very lucky if it gets press coverage which seems, on its own terms, fair. Perversely, it is likely to get most coverage if it can exploit general, rather than politically related, news values. The style of British journalism means that, outside the small circulation broadsheet papers, the personality-based parties with simple policies can be most easily projected. None of this may be surprising, but perhaps it shows up an inconsistency in the approach of the press to elections. Regardless of the cruder forms of party bias, newspapers all seem to treat general elections as processes of rational political debate, in which there are, by definition, 'issues' that tidily divide the parties and on which clear cut rival 'policies' can be presented. Intemperate electioneering is disapproved. At root, newspapers seem to expect politicians – and voters – to have reasons for their views and to argue them out. It is the minor party's lot, simply because it is not yet big, to be largely excluded from that model of electoral politics. If anything, the model flatters the rationality of the major parties and their voters. Exclusion might on that ground seem not just bad luck but an affront.

Notes: Chapter 9

Colin Seymour-Ure and Adrian Smith are at the University of Kent.

1 A long interview of John Tyndall in *The Times* (30 August 1977), in response to a Front 'challenge' about media publicity, avoided trouble with the NUJ by being balanced with a Socialist Workers' Party feature the following day. In September and October 1978 the activities of the Anti-Nazi League and the Campaign Against Racism in the Media attracted increasing attention (*The Times*, 22 September 1978; *Sunday Times*, 1 October 1978; etc.).

2 'Our policy of prominent street demonstrations and noisy marches has been necessary because of the refusal of the media to give us an opportunity to put across our views', John Tyndall, quoted in *The Times* (30 August 1977).

3 Press coverage of them is obtainable from Adrian Smith.

The Media: Discussion

Kellner/Worcester

Paul McKee (Independent Television News)
One of the most interesting developments over the last few years has been the amount of coverage that the *Sun* has given to polls not just within the election campaign, but also in the couple of years previously. If you add up the number of column inches devoted to polls in the *Sun*, it would probably be larger than for any other newspaper, in absolute as well as proportional terms. There have been some enormous double-page spreads in the *Sun*.

Bruce Page
Getting a few words into a couple of pages.

Paul McKee
Well yes, but a lot more tables too. The *Sun* and the *News of the World* certainly ran more poll stories in the election campaign than ever before. What's been interesting has been the way the polls have featured so large in that group of papers. The *Mirror* has devoted very little space to polls. I wonder if you could make any general, speculative comment on that?

Bob Worcester
On 26 April we asked 'Have you seen the results of any opinion polls recently saying how people say they'll vote at the next election?'; if yes – 'Which companies were they conducted by?': 22 per cent said Yes, Gallup; 16 per cent said Yes, MORI; 15 per cent Yes, Marplan. We cross-tabulated that by newspaper readership. *Sun* newspaper readers are only marginally more likely to recall Marplan than Gallup, MORI, or NOP. I don't know whether I'm measuring the message or the medium but Marplan's not getting across as well among *Sun* readers as Gallup is among *Telegraph* readers, MORI among *Express* readers, or NOP among *Mail* readers.

Peter Kellner
Can I respond as a journalist? I think Paul McKee is right. I'm not now making any comment on Walter Terry's appalling write-up of polls during the election but I think the *Sun* and the *News of the World*, not for the first time, showed a much shrewder understanding of the capacity of their readers to absorb numerical information than many other papers. I instance three things, one of which is a prejudice. The first point is that if you look at the sporting coverage of any popular newspaper it is dense with the most complex tables most of which I wouldn't begin to try and understand (mainly because I take no interest in horse racing). Clearly, very large numbers of people do follow in minute detail quite complex, small-type numerical presentations. It seems to me daft to assume that many of those people won't follow larger print, poll table stories. The counterpoint to that is that on the *Sunday Times*,

which I would have thought ought to have a greater respect for the intelligence of its readers, my perpetual battle is to prevent six-column pictures. Recently we ran more than a half-page story on a poll on the police. About half the space was taken up by a picture of policemen which told you nothing that you couldn't have learned in about a tenth of the space. There was one table. The third point I'll make is my explanation and my prejudice. I just think journalists as a breed are infinitely less numerate than the majority of our customers.

Bob Worcester

Could I also show a Gallup Poll finding which I think is very interesting? On 2–3 May Gallup asked 'Have you seen or heard the results of an opinion poll in the last few days? Do you remember which party the poll said was in the lead? Was that a big lead or a small lead?' The power of television I think is very evident here. Big lead for Conservatives, 4 per cent (*Observer* readers?); small lead for Conservatives, 32 per cent; neck and neck, 6 per cent; small lead for Labour, 25 per cent; big lead for Labour, none. Now, the *Mail* isn't read by 25 per cent of the population; they got that from Sunday night's television, I suspect. So you have a lot of people paying pretty close attention.

Peter Pulzer

A very brief point. In fact, a hypothesis as to why more people appear to recall Gallup Polls than any other. It may just be that Gallup is a generic term rather than a brand name, rather in the manner of Kleenex.

Gordon Heald (Gallup)

It's in the *Oxford Dictionary*, so it must be a word.

Paul McKee

I would give the wooden spoon for poll coverage to the *Sun* for headlines, but in terms of the information they've presented over three or four years, they get the first prize.

Bruce Page

One of the most interesting things for a journalist to hear touched on is the curious attitude of papers to poll presentations. Remarkably interesting that it should be the *Sun* and the *News of the World*, exactly as Peter Kellner says at the bottom of the market, which assume numeracy in their readers. When I took over the *New Statesman* a couple of years ago, it was a rule among the journalists that no information depending on tables or numbers could be presented, because the readers couldn't take it. I took the view that it was impossible to produce any sort of up-to-date journal dealing with serious politics that way. But the journalists act as 'gate-keepers', as censors, and the oddity is the higher up you go in a paper's readership profile, the more viciously anti-numerate the journalists are.

Paul McKee

That's exactly our experience from a television viewpoint. Over the last five or six years, we've taken a deliberate policy of trying to pack in more and more information. This is particularly true of our election results coverage, which is essentially all about numbers. We've had no negative reactions at all from that. If anything, it's been the other way round in terms of both audience figures, and viewers' reactions.

John Barter (NOP)
My complaint about the papers is that they say they don't want to produce tables and then they put the numbers in the narrative where nobody sees them.

Pilsworth/Harrison

Hugh Berrington (University of Newcastle), Chairman
Both Martin Harrison and Michael Pilsworth do lay some emphasis on the sheer unpopularity of the length of election coverage. So it seems to me that there is some kind of tension here between what one might define as the electorate on the one hand, and the television audience on the other. Somewhere in your mind is some notion of serving the electorate, some definition of what service to the electorate involves, but it's a definition that might not be generally accepted.

Martin Harrison
The chairman has made a point that academic critics of television are prone to forget; namely, that there is a limited capacity for digestion among the television audience and the electorate for this sort of material. We can't really expect the election to get more coverage than it does at the moment. Within that constraint, I think that concern for the audience implies a style of coverage which is more questioning and analytical. I thought that both channels recognised this to some extent in 1979. They shifted the balance from simply reporting events to helping the viewer to understand what the issues were and what the policies of the various parties were towards the issues.

Michael Pilsworth (London Weekend Television)
Yes, obviously that is the central question. During the 1979 campaign, the problem that the broadcasters faced was how to cover the campaign in ways that they found professionally satisfying. Underneath the statement that it was a quiet campaign, there was an anxiety among broadcasters that they had been hemmed in by the strategies used by the parties in setting up campaign events. Lying behind Hugh Berrington's question, though, is a deeper one: who decides what values the broadcasters should employ if they are to refrain from just accepting what is provided for them by the parties? I mentioned ITN's technique of carrying out a poll to find out what people thought the main issues were and then trying to relate those issues to the manifestos. That perhaps is an example of one way round the problem. Another approach is that adopted by programmes like *Weekend World*, which aim to cover topics at much greater length though for a much smaller audience. The key point is that audience appreciation indices are always very high for programmes such as *Weekend World* which deal seriously with issues, higher than for most other campaign coverage. Given that people do not want to engage themselves

everyday in finding out what Jim and Maggie have been doing on the campaign trail, and that they do find coverage of these kind of repetitious events rather tedious, the question is how to overcome that without getting involved in 'producerism', where the broadcasters lay themselves open to the charge that they are determining the issues and the conduct of the campaign. The correct course, I think, lies somewhere between those two extremes.

Peter Kellner

Trying to compare your experiences with those of a print journalist, we seem to inhabit very different worlds. Nobody would ever try to construct a newspaper in anything like the same way that you produce television programmes, with your hang-ups about doing deals with the parties and your concern to measure everything to the second. The oddity is that we need politicians more than they need us, while they need you more than you need them. So, if anything, one would expect newspapers to be more beholden to politicians than television companies. I would like, if I may, to turn Michael Pilsworth's comments about 'producerism' on their head and suggest that the broadcasters should engage in *more* agenda-setting. Because to me an election is a point in time which relates the last five years to the next five. Every election is a potential revolution; it is an event concerning policies, ideologies and the impact of government on people's lives. But as determined by politicians and reflected on television and also to a large extent in the press, the event is about the personalities of the day. So I wonder whether there is a case for us all, but especially television, stepping back and saying we are going to concentrate a lot less on day-to-day events – the holding of lambs and all that rubbish. Why don't you be bold and say, 'well, I don't care if all the popular dailies are going to have these pictures on their front pages tomorrow morning, this is not what the election is about. We are actually going to devote another two minutes to counter-inflation policies and two minutes less to Margaret Thatcher holding a lamb'.

Paul McKee

I want to take up Martin Harrison's point about the unpopularity of election coverage. This is an oft-repeated phrase for which the evidence is difficult to find. Looking at the viewing figures for our bulletins over the last election campaign (and remember this was an unusually long campaign), the average daily audience was significantly above the same weeks in 1978, with the exception of those *News at Ten* bulletins which did not start until 10.15 p.m. In other words, there was no evidence of an increasing 'switch-off' factor. Another piece of evidence is the small survey which Mallory Wober (IBA) did in London. This asked questions about how interesting and helpful different kinds of election coverage were. When the proportion saying unhelpful is subtracted from the proportion saying helpful, this gives a net score of $+35$ for news bulletins, $+27$ for current-affairs programmes and $+5$ for PEBs. In terms of the interesting/boring dimension, the scores are $+6$ for news bulletins, $+10$ for current-affairs programmes and -31 for PEBs. As far as I can see, there is no evidence in viewing figures, post-election surveys or audience-appreciation indices to show that election coverage is uninteresting or unpopular with the audience.

On the lack of innovation in election coverage, certainly the major factor why ITN's coverage in 1979 in many respects resembled that of October 1974 was the minority Parliament. A number of us spent three wasted summers on election preparations for the following autumn, elections which never came about. If you are going to get major innovations in election coverage, you do need a gap in between the elections, so that you can as it were empty the nesting store and fill it back up again. I think this is a more important point than the institutional constraints stressed by Michael Pilsworth. At the same time, however, I think Michael underplayed the significance of one specific constraint: section 9 of the RPA. This legal constraint means that in covering constituency contests, we cannot admit the existence of a contest until nominations close, and even when nominations close any candidate has a veto on a constituency report. Now I agree that the Marshall judgement defining 'taking part' was an important one, though in practice we were in any case edging our way round this problem. But this is why the BBC and ourselves are pressing the Home Office like nobody's business to see if it is possible to get rid of section 9 or at least amend it significantly.

Austin Mitchell
A large section of the audience couldn't care two stuffs about the election. In fact, they find the election too long and too boring. In this kind of situation, the broadcasters are conspicuously lacking in courage. They allow themselves to be bullied far too much by the political parties, so that the election turns into a cosy conspiracy between the broadcasters and the increasingly media-oriented parties. When the broadcasters congratulated themselves at the end of the campaign that there had been no major problems, that's because they had given way all along the line. In this cosy conspiracy the two groups which suffer are, first, the audience, which should perhaps be served up with the truth, and secondly the Labour Party. One problem was that we should have been asking the questions of an opposition which really had no answers. In other words, the Labour Party should have taken the initiative and been on the attack. We lost the initiative partly through our own fault because Percy Clarke (Labour Party Publicity Director) was too much of a gentleman in negotiating the times of the press conferences. The result is they finished up at the same time. Instead of us getting up an hour earlier and taking the initiative, the coverage of the campaign on television became a kind of drinks dispenser. Without even having to press a button, you got a cup of black and a cup of white. It was dispensed automatically every news bulletin, complete with automatic feed and balance. So we were never allowed to put the questions, to seize the initiative. You would ask the questions and you would get a picture of Mrs Thatcher holding a calf. You would ask more questions and you would get a picture of her holding two shopping bags outside a super-market. All you got in answer to your questions was sickly grins from the other side, an infuriating situation to be placed in.

Mallory Wober (Independent Broadcasting Authority)
Two serious problems. First, television is not just an organ for providing information, but is also quite clearly an organ for articulating emotions with the public. We have had no discussion whatsoever yet on how this latter

function should be approached. Secondly, there is to my mind an incorrect assumption that the television audience is homogeneous and that viewers are equal. Viewers include people with an IQ of 160 at the top and 20 per cent at the bottom, by definition, have an IQ of less than 80. Now, how do you provide a programme which informs the public when 20 per cent of them have IQs of 80 or less? It is really a very challenging task and I have no idea what one should recommend.

Richard Rose (University of Strathclyde)
A point from Scotland. Michael Pilsworth mentioned, but didn't really dwell on the implications of, the fact that a British general election is no longer a single election as measured by a common 'Con–Lab–Lib' pattern of contestation. It was quite obvious in 1979 that the broadcasting of the Scottish contest was an exercise of straight power which, in fact, ignored the peculiar regional structure of the IBA, and also of course proved what a nonsense BBC Scotland was. Balance, in other words, has a territorial dimension. And what do you do with the twelve formerly Labour MPs who may be fighting the next election as Social Democrats?

Paul Whiteley (University of Bristol)
I can understand Michael Pilsworth feeling constrained by the legal requirements that are placed on television but the requirements are none the less important. As far as election coverage is concerned, the press is biased. With the obvious exception of the *Mirror*, newspapers are pro-Conservative in varying degrees, though this varies from unconscious bias to outright manipulation of news and comment which would do justice to a leader writer for *Pravda*. If there weren't such legal restraints on television, I suspect these same biases would creep into television. That is why these legal restraints exist, and that is why we have them.

Karl-Peter Markl (West Germany)
In reply to Mallory Wober's comment about the restricted capacity of the television audience, we have to ask not only 'in what way?', but also 'who by?' Who is it who restricts? Who is it who talks of restrictive capacity? And for what purposes? Whose interests does this serve politically?

Bob Self

Richard Rose
The *Granada 500* programmes must have cost a hell of a lot of money. I would be interested in the explanation for Granada's investment decision.

Bob Self
The *Granada 500* worked out quite cheap as television goes. Compared to the cost of a film or a soap opera, this wasn't an expensive investment in television terms. It wasn't simply a ritual either. It was regarded as a serious and important attempt to permit the electorate of a particular constituency to ask

the questions that concerned them to people who could provide them with answers: the panel of experts in the local programmes and then the party leaders in the final programme. And in that respect the programme seems to be an interesting and useful innovation in television election coverage. It certainly gets away from the ritualised debates in which a well-known television interviewer flays one or other of the party leaders. And the audience ratings show that whatever people learned from it, they did at least watch it and must therefore have been interested in it. So I don't think we can dismiss the *Granada 500* completely out of hand simply because the idea had been used in earlier elections.

David Lipsey (former political adviser to Prime Minister Callaghan)
You said that having party leaders faced by voters was the beginning of an era. I think that the *Granada 500* programme is the end of an era. Because I have heard your interpretation, I see the strength in it, and it is very dangerous. I was involved with the Callaghan campaign, and it is of course very dangerous for those who are involved to be critical of programmes. But I am the least paranoid of individuals about television and about newspaper reports, and it is I think very very rare for bias to exist when an interview has been conducted by a special interviewer. But if I did not know that David Kemp, the *Granada 500* producer, is a man of quite unimpeachable integrity, I would say that the programme was the most hideous fix. That is how it would appear to me, if I did not know the people involved. There is no way that a politician can argue on television, if you have a nurse in the front row, a sweet little girl of 17, saying that she is paid whatever she said she was paid a week. There it is, it looks sweet, it is televisually appealing and there is no way that the most superb political performer in the world can argue against that kind of visual impact. The fact was that the leader of the opposition, in contrast, was tossed a series of extremely soft balls to hit to all parts of the ballpark. That's the nature of the programme, and that's why I don't think this kind of television is going to work. And so I must say in all frankness that any Labour adviser who again advised his leader to go on a programme of that character would in the light of the experience last time be acting very irresponsibly to his own party. Certainly, I could never advise anybody that I was involved with to go on a programme of that character again.

Bob Self
I do agree with you about the impact of the nurse sitting in the front row, but Callaghan handled her question very badly. He gave a very aggressive and unnecessarily irritable retort when he could have answered the question more gently. Again, I would agree that Mrs Thatcher had much easier questions overall. The audience howled with approval when in reply to a question on immigration she said that she would refuse to let fiancés in. And it took a couple of minutes before the audience clapping died down when she said she had in the past and would in the future vote for capital punishment. But I'm not sure it's 'irresponsible' to allow electors to ask questions of the people who hope to represent them, who hope indeed to be their next Prime Minister.

On a more practical note, suppose David Lipsey were adviser to the Leader of the Opposition at the next election; suppose too that the leader felt that he was quite strong in this sort of confrontation, and that his party were behind in the polls. I am not sure that under these circumstances David would say 'we shouldn't do this because it would be irresponsible'. David or some other adviser would say: 'we have a chance here to pull back some very valuable points in the opinion polls by flaying the Prime Minister with her own record.' We will benefit too from the fact that the Leader of the Opposition will be participating in the same programme as the Prime Minister and will, therefore, be raised to her level.

Geoffrey Alderman (Royal Holloway College, University of London)
Could I disagree profoundly with David Lipsey? In the early 1950s we had a series of the most artificial of interviews with politicians imaginable, where not only did politicians ask to see the questions beforehand, but in some cases actually wrote the questions themselves. Now the politicians have got to make a choice: are they or are they not prepared to face the people who elect them?

Bonnie Angelo (*Time* magazine)
Have you given any thought to the rather hard grid format that has evolved in the USA? There, the candidates are all present at the same time. In the first half a panel of three or four journalists asks questions which go to each of the candidates in turn, while in the second half the questions come from the audience, but still going to all the candidates.

Bob Self
Somebody observed the 1976 presidential debates for Granada. The feeling then was that the debates were very theatrical, very staged, with an exceptionally hushed audience. Rather like a joint press conference, I think.

Bonnie Angelo
It was not a debate in the sense of candidates attacking each other head on. None the less, the candidates were responding to the same questions.

Peter Kellner
As a journalist, it is part of my profession to interview people, though not in front of the cameras. If one has a difficult interviewee, it will often take five, ten, or twenty questions covering five, ten, or twenty minutes to make a particular point. Now, it strikes me that in the 1979 election I can't remember a single important fact that was produced by any interview, whether professional or, in the case of your programme, amateur. I recall from the EEC referendum that you broke away from this format and took a coach-load of Granada citizens around the Common Market. You filmed hours and hours with partisans from each side going round French farms and Belgian steel-mills, trying thereby to get some more subtle and deeper idea of what was going on in the Common Market. I found the evolution of ordinary people's attitudes as they were confronted by all this completely compelling, convincing and authentic. Perhaps you should consider employing this technique in a general election, using your 500 not in a wholly artificial studio manner, but using film to try and get at the way campaign events affect ordinary people.

Seymour-Ure/Smith

Ivor Crewe
What does Colin Seymour-Ure think the correct treatment of the minor parties by the media should be? If we had to write a memo advising the editor of one of the popular newspapers, how would we define fair and correct treatment of the candidate of the Go to Blazes Party? How would that differ from the treatment such candidates actually got?

Colin Seymour-Ure
Generally speaking, make sure you find out what their own evaluation of themselves is and do your best to include some kind of summary of their own evaluation of themselves in your own coverage. In more specific terms there are obviously at least two problems here. First, there's the question of whether you mention minor parties at all, and I agree that there isn't much justification for referring to a lot of them, particularly the ones that stand in only one constituency. And then, secondly, there's the question of how you actually cope with the ones you do cover. It would be easier to write a short brief for a newspaper with suggestions about how they might appropriately be covered than it would be to offer criteria for covering them at all that are in any obvious sense more sensible than those currently adopted.

Mallory Wober
What I feel is valuable in your paper is something like an elitist anthropological level of analysis which enables you to dispense with all your tables and say 'my feel for it is that the tabloid press has treated the minor parties badly'. That comes across. In a way, that's a useful level of analysis which is not frequently applied to television and particularly not by skilled operators. I just wish that it was done. We have to feel for it and encourage people to do it.

Paul McKee
The most memorable treatment, I think, of the minor parties – and the most effective – was the Workers' Revolutionary Party's five-minute party election broadcast. The audience for that was something like 20 million across all three networks. It was the plainest, simplest PEB ever. Corin Redgrave, straight into camera. Unbelievably effective. The way in which he coolly and calmly talked about the decline of the capitalist system. You blinked at the words that were coming out – at his calm, reflective presentation. Extremely effective. In terms of people's information about the WRP, that PEB conveyed more information to more people than the whole of the rest of their coverage both on television, and in the press.

Bob Worcester
And, of course, he didn't trivialise his own message. There was no 'gatekeeper'.

Paul McKee
That PEB enabled him to present his own assessment of what they were offering. Going on to the presentation of the minor parties in news bulletins or current-affairs bulletins, I don't think that by and large they were trivialised.

There were a number of interviews; the manifestos were reported, though as Martin Harrison said the manifestos were perhaps compressed beyond acceptable levels. But my impression is they got a very, very fair crack of the whip.

Adrian Smith
When I used the term 'trivialisation', I was referring specifically to coverage of the parties on the revolutionary left. In fact, it's interesting that you mentioned the WRP broadcast, because Margaret Foreword, the *Sun*'s TV critic, compared Corin Redgrave's broadcast with his earlier roles in 1960s soap operas. She was very, very dismissive.

Paul McKee
I don't think that was a typical reaction.

Martin Harrison
On the television point, I would agree with what Paul McKee has said, I don't think television did trivialise – except, let's face it, some things *are* trivial. For me, Auberon Waugh is trivial, and a serious treatment of Auberon Waugh in Devon North just did not seem to me to be good journalism. There was of course (apart from the PEB) the *Hustings* programme. Though a small-audience programme, the WRP and I think the SNP all got a pretty good run – and one which wasn't heavily edited either. So if you were willing to be an insomniac, yes, you could get it. Somewhere on the network, it was there.

Part Four

The Polls and Psephology

10

'Improving, but Could Do Better': the Media and the Polls in the 1979 General Election

IVOR CREWE

The polls and the media, at least at election time, cannot live without the other. The polls depend on the press and broadcasting for payment and publicity. And the media depend on the polls to provide copy – not only as feature and background stories but, increasingly, as the 'hard' news of the campaign. But as for many couples, living together is almost as difficult as living apart. For what the media and polls most need from the other is what each finds most difficult to provide. The media, as always, demand speed; but high-quality opinion polling requires the organisation of a far-flung labour force and attention to detail – in other words, time. The media demand simplicity, certainty and brevity; but poll findings are often ambivalent, and their correct interpretation requires balance, qualification and elaboration. British elections are often close-run, so the media demand pin-point precision; but the most carefully designed and executed poll is subject to sampling and other sources of error. The media, especially the financially pressed newspapers, demand cut-price service; but polls are labour- and petrol-intensive and so cannot be cheap. Above all, the media have an insatiable demand for news, but the polls strive after truth, and the truth is not always newsworthy.

However frayed the relationship, the polls and the media need each other enough to compromise. This paper is about the form that compromise took in the last general election campaign. It seeks answers to four questions:

(1) What kind of polls did the media commission?
(2) How imaginative and effective was their use of these?
(3) How accurately were they reported?
(4) What was the impact of these reports on the electorate?

What Kind of Polls Did the Media Commission?

In any industry the virtues and vices of intense competition are the same: on the one hand, the promise of innovation, efficiency and value for money; on the other, the risk of corner-cutting and a deterioration in quality. So it was with the polls in April and May 1979.

On the credit side there was, first, a remarkable *profusion* of polls. The standard poll is a 'one-off' survey of the whole of the national electorate (excluding Northern Ireland). But as well as 'one-offs' there were panel surveys, a time-series survey and a 'call-back', that is, a single wave of re-interviews. In addition to surveys of Britain, there were polls of Scotland and London, of a hundred 'key marginals', of Liberal-held seats, of thirteen 'barometer seats' and of single constituencies including three in the West Midlands and nine in Wales. And to add to analyses of the whole electorate there were polls of special groups, including first-time voters, 'young Mums' and National Front sympathisers. It is difficult to believe that such a variety of focus and design would have occurred without the spur of Fleet Street rivalry.

Secondly, most of the polls were a tribute to the companies' organisational ingenuity. Of the twenty-eight polls, seven completed their fieldwork within a day, and another fourteen within two days. The average gap between completion of interviewing and publication of results (if the Sunday press is excluded) was thirty-six hours. But it was not uncommon for some initial findings to be made public on the same day as the fieldwork. Once again, it is hard not to attribute that degree of organisational efficiency to the pressure of competition among the media and the polling companies.

On the debit side, however, was a decline in the quality of the typical sample – in its size, selection method and probable margin of error. As Table 10.1 shows, the average sample size (1,323) had slipped yet further from its October 1974 level (1,513) which, in turn, was considerably lower than that for February 1974 (2,118). The main reason was an increase in the number of one-day or two-day 'quickies' (from twelve in October 1974 to twenty-one in May 1979) which, from pressure of time, tend to be based on smaller samples. Never before had so many campaign polls been conducted on samples of 1,000, give or take a hundred. But there was no evidence of a compensating increase in the number of sampling points: the result must have therefore been an increase in the typical poll's sampling error.

In reply to this implied criticism, the polling companies undoubtedly have one compelling retort. Of the five final polls, three predicted the share of the vote going to each of the three main parties to within 1 per cent of the actual result; of these, two (the MORI polls

Table 10.1 *Aspects of the Design of Opinion Polls in the 1970,
February 1974, October 1974 and 1979 General Elections*

	1970	February 1974	October 1974	1979
Number of national polls in campaign	25	22	23	28
Number with fieldwork conducted within one day	n.a.	n.a.	8	7
Number with fieldwork conducted within two days	n.a.	n.a.	4	14
Average sample size (mean)	1,959	2,118	1,513	1,448*
Number with samples of less than 1,100	4	1	7	12

Notes:
*This drops to 1,323 if the ITN and BBC surveys, of which there was no equivalent in earlier elections, are omitted.
Sources:
D. E. Butler and M. Pinto-Duschinsky, *British General Election of 1970* (London: Macmillan, 1971), p. 178; D. E. Butler and D. Kavanagh, *British General Election of February 1974* (London: Macmillan, 1974), p. 95; D. E. Butler and D. Kavanagh, *British General Election of October 1974* (London: Macmillan, 1975), pp. 190–1; D. E. Butler and D. Kavanagh, *British General Election of 1979* (London: Macmillan, 1980), p. 264.

for the *Evening Standard* and for the *Daily Express*) used samples of 947 and 1,089, respectively; and the latter was conducted entirely on one day. Moreover, the least accurate of these five polls, Gallup's for the *Daily Telegraph*, was based on 2,348 interviews spread over three days. Indeed, it could be argued further that as the essence of an accurate election forecast is the conducting of fieldwork on the eve or day of polling itself, anything other than a short interview based on a sample of limited size is impractical.

How Imaginative and Effective Was the Media's Use of the Polls?

The major drawback to the 'quickies' did not lie in their accuracy, but in the limited uses to which they could be put. They provided valuable 'horse-race' copy – stories on the party lead, the ratings of the party leaders and the relative importance of the major issues. But they could not be used for much else. Pressure of time necessitates not only a small sample, but a short interview, and this in turn severely restricts both the number of questions and their nature. It excludes, for example, open-ended and multiple-choice questions; rules out all but the simplest of analyses; and precludes the examination of crucial sub-samples, such as the 'don't knows' or respondents in marginal seats or a particular region. Thus the newspapers which normally relied on short, quickie polls – the *Sun, Daily Express, Daily Mail* and *Evening Standard* – published stories with the same, predictable format of party lead, ratings of party leaders and importance of issues. Despite the breathless style in which these stories were often written, they soon got dull.

As if the constraints of the short, quickie poll were not limiting enough, the media also failed to make imaginative or effective enough use of what poll material they had. Space restricts me to three examples.

(1) COMPARISONS WITH THE PREVIOUS ELECTION

Except for reminders to readers that in both 1970 and February 1974 parties had recovered from positions almost as unpromising as Labour's in 1979, the media did not use poll material from previous elections. Yet to do so would have been simple and cheap and added considerably to the range and sophistication of poll stories. For example, in order to explain shifts of party support, as opposed simply to measuring them, references to the state of opinion at the previous election are essential. An illustration of what can go wrong without making such references back is the interpretation put on the electoral implications of the importance of different issues. Throughout the campaign the most important issue was prices; and by the final week Labour was the preferred party on it, especially among those citing it as important. The general conclusion was that this must help Labour's chances. A more qualified judgement might have been made had it been noticed that prices was also the single most important issue in October 1974, but to a much greater extent, so that by 1979 it had, in fact, sharply *declined* in salience. Similarly, less stress might have been put on Labour's edge over the Conservatives as the best party for dealing with unemployment, had it been realised that its advantage on the issue had dropped considerably since October 1974.

(2) LEADERSHIP RATINGS

Before the campaign, the polls asked separate questions on the popularity of each of the three main parties' leader. But during the campaign, except for some Marplan polls, the question on the popularity of the party leaders was always a minor variation of 'Who would make the better Prime Minister, Mr Callaghan, Mrs Thatcher or Mr Steel?' In other words, respondents were invited to make a relative assessment, and always in terms of the best Prime Minister.

Yet this question reveals nothing about the absolute level of a party leader's popularity. The fact that in these popularity stakes Mrs Thatcher consistently trailed Mr Callaghan during the campaign might have taken on less significance in the media had somebody examined her pre-campaign absolute 'ratings' and noticed that they had persistently been higher than those of Mr Heath in *his* opposition years up to the 1970 election – which, moreover, he won.

(3) ISSUE SALIENCE

It is notoriously difficult to measure accurately the relative importance of different issues in determining the vote. None the less, there is one respect in which the polls could readily have improved their coverage of issue salience: by distinguishing between the public as a whole, and the 'issue public' – those who specifically mentioned the issue as important. It can certainly make a difference to the party lead on an issue. For example, the BBC election-day survey found that among the public as a whole the Conservatives held a narrow 3 per cent lead over Labour on industrial relations but an equally slender 3 per cent deficit on unemployment. The natural conclusion to draw was that on both issues the parties were running almost neck and neck. But among those for whom the issues mattered, party preferences were far from evenly balanced: the Conservatives led by 15 per cent on industrial relations but trailed by 15 per cent on unemployment.

The result of these various shortcomings, I suggest, was that the media extracted plenty of copy from the polls, including front-page headlines, but few genuinely good stories, that is, information that threw new and important light on the electorate's thinking. The exceptions worth singling out are the two panel surveys by Marplan and MORI, although here the originality lay more in the sampling design than in the questions or analysis; and, more deserving of laurels, the RSL poll for the *Observer* on 22 April. Here was one story which added to our knowledge about the public's thinking and suggested a new way of examining the impact of party policies, all with the aid of a few simple questions about the relative popularity and likely success of the policy proposals of the major parties.

The Accuracy of the Media's Poll Reports

There is continual controversy about the 'accuracy of the polls'. But what the reader or viewer sees is not the bare poll statistics, but their presentation by the media, packaged in headlines, interpretative text, charts and tables. How accurate was that presentation in 1979?

Though the press rarely defaulted on its obligation to publish the technical details of the polls it reported, the media were guilty of one major, and almost certainly deliberate sin – the failure to take sampling error into account when assessing the significance of the party lead in the polls, and, more important, of changes in the party lead from one poll to the next. This cannot be attributed to technical innocence. Early in the campaign a number of journalists cited sampling error as a possible explanation for the apparent discrepancies between the polls, and some (for instance, Michael Evans in the *Daily Express* and Robert Carvel in the *Evening Standard*) wrote separate pieces explaining in simple language the importance of taking sampling error into account when interpreting the polls. But the public had to wait until a week before polling day for *The Economist* to point out that the whole of the apparent movement in polls over the previous week could be attributed to errors in sampling rather than to changed intentions by the voters.

Combined with other ambiguities in the data, the possible effects of sampling error were systematically ignored, in order to give the impression that the gap between the parties was slowly closing and could be expected to narrow further. The constant implication, and not infrequent assertion, was that it would be a close finish – obviously the most newsworthy outcome for the media. In the first fortnight of the campaign, when the Conservative lead in the polls stayed stubbornly high at 11 per cent on average, the media used two devices to suggest a narrowing gap: first, comparisons back to the Conservatives' much greater leads in January and February, when the winter's strikes were at their height; and secondly, to alleged expectations, attributed to nobody in particular, that the gap was bound to narrow. A good example is Gordon Greig's report on 6 April for the *Daily Mail*:

The Tories go into the general election campaign with a lead of only 6 per cent over Labour . . . a special National Opinion Poll survey this morning shows a sizeable drop in Tory support after months of strikes and industrial turmoil had seemed to leave Labour without hope of recovery. The findings of NOP suggested that the next four weeks will decide who is going to win. The past three general elections have all been won or lost during the campaign after the polls had fluctuated wildly. And that looks like happening again.

By the penultimate week of the campaign, when with hindsight there indeed appeared to be a narrowing of the gap, the press eagerly seized on the evidence without pausing to make the counter-qualifications it had included earlier when the polls pointed the other way. The *Daily*

Express began its 25 April front-page story on MORI's 6 per cent Conservative lead with: 'The Tories are now facing the Week of the Big Squeeze [how did it know?] with their lead over Labour getting smaller and smaller [where was the evidence?].' The 6 per cent lead was described as 'a dramatic drop from last week's 12 per cent' (with no mention of the 10 per cent lead given by the previous MORI poll).

By election day the *Sun*'s interpretation of the four final polls, despite three which put the Conservative lead between 5·6 per cent and 7 per cent, was 'It's Maggie by a whisker' – almost certainly a deliberate attempt to frighten wavering Conservatives into turning out and staying loyal.

The media's artificial generation of excitement was a distortion of the polls. Its widespread, self-reinforcing pattern made it more than casual misreporting. But it amounted to less than fabrication, because there was a basis of reality to the press reports, even if that reality was systematically exaggerated. It undoubtedly owed more to considerations of news value than of partisan advantage. None the less, as we shall see, it was not without partisan consequences, however unintended.

The Impact of Poll Reports on the Electorate

Misreporting of polls in the media would not be a serious matter, if people took no notice of them. Are the polls read? If so, are their results remembered? And if so, do they influence the way people vote?

Valid evidence is hard to come by, and what little exists is inconclusive. The safest conclusion is that the polls do have an impact but neither a strong nor consistent one. If the polls produced a strong 'bandwagon' effect – that is, persuaded the undecided to support the party with an early lead – one would expect that lead to widen steadily as the campaign progressed. Alternatively, if the polls produced a strong 'underdog' effect, one would expect that lead to narrow steadily. Neither pattern has consistently or even often occurred in postwar elections. However, the polls' impact could be weaker or more fleeting. For example, the polls' overestimate of the margin of the winning party in eight out of the ten postwar elections up to October 1974 has led to the suggestion that it does have an underdog effect, but only on last-minute deciders. Without survey evidence, there is no way of telling for sure.

Some new and direct evidence (see Table 10.2), based on Gallup's election-day survey for BBC television, shows that two out of three electors (and a higher proportion of voters) claimed to have 'seen or heard the results of an opinion poll'. But only 2 per cent admitted that their vote was influenced as a result. This tiny figure can be challenged on the grounds that some respondents will have been unaware of the polls' influence on them, or if aware of it, unwilling to say so. On the other hand, the figure might be exaggerating the true number by including some who would have voted the same way irrespective of the polls. The estimate of 2 per cent is probably as good as any available. Analysis of their vote is hampered by small numbers but does offer tentative support for the underdog thesis. Among those who noticed the polls but denied being affected, the Conservatives had a 15 per cent majority; among the tiny minority who admitted to being influenced, Labour had an 11 per cent majority.

Summary and Conclusions

On the basis of the foregoing account I should like to propound three linked propositions about the way the polls are reported in Britain.

PROPOSITION 1

However static public opinion actually is, the polls enable the media to give an impression of flux, change and excitement.

This is because sampling error alone, especially for relatively small and highly clustered samples, will produce fluctuations in the poll statistics, the news value of which will be too great to suppress in the interests of technical purity. A rider can, therefore, be added.

Rider to Proposition 1

The more polls there are, the more true this is. This is because the incidence of rogue polls (for example, the one-in-twenty outside the 95 per cent probability limit) will be higher, as will the variation in sampling methods, fieldwork operations, question wording, procedures for dealing with 'don't knows' and other components of 'agency effects'.

PROPOSITION 2

However clear the outcome and trend, polls allow the media to hedge its bets.

This comes about through a happy coincidence of news values and technical considerations. It is to the media's advantage to protect itself against possible error, to provide some balance by comforting the likely losers and warning the likely winners among its readership, and

Table 10.2 *Whether Public Noticed Polls, and Were Influenced by Them, by May 1979 Vote*

(n =)	All (1,940)	Did not notice polls (559)	Noticed polls but not influenced (1,293)	Noticed polls and also influenced (44)	Noticed polls, influenced, and decided vote late (10)
May 1979 vote	%	%	%	%	%
Conservative	46	39	49	34	(5)
Labour	38	47	34	45	(2)
Liberal	14	11	15	20	(3)
Other	2	3	2	–	(–)
	100%	100%	100%	100%	
Conservative Lead	+8%	–8%	+15%	–11%	
Proportion of all respondents	100%	31%	64%	2%	0·4%

Note:
The questions were: 'Have you seen or heard the results of an opinion poll in the last few days?' and 'When you finally decided which way to vote, were you influenced at all by what the opinion polls were saying?'; *n* refers to the column percentage base and does not correspond exactly with the bottom row percentages which include non-voters.

Source:
Gallup/Essex survey for BBC television, 2–3 May 1980 (quota sample, Great Britain, *n* = 2,435).

to give the impression of a close and unpredictable result. And the sources of genuine ambiguity in interpreting the poll results provide all the justification needed for reporting this way. Again, one can therefore add a rider.

Rider to Proposition 2

The more polls there are, the easier it is to hedge bets. Propositions 1 and 2 lead to a third.

PROPOSITION 3

However improbable a poll finding is, the media will always publish (broadcast) it.

This is not only because of the media's natural wish for a return on their investment, but because the sources of ambiguity mentioned earlier can always be speculatively cited in justification (at least for a time). Once again, the more polls there are, the more true the proposition is, because figures neighbouring on the rogue findings are more likely to be available, thus saving it from appearing too out of line. An excellent illustration was the *Observer*'s continued publication of its RSL polls without even a reduction in the length or prominence of coverage, long after it was clear that, for reasons never satisfactorily established, they were markedly exaggerating the Conservative lead. Indeed, to this proposition one can also add a rider.

Rider to Proposition 3

The more improbable a poll finding, the more likely the media will give it prominence. This is so because, on top of the factors that enable the media to treat almost any poll finding seriously, at least for a short period, the most startling findings are, obviously enough, the hottest news.

What changes, then, might reduce the kind of misreporting described in this chapter? Should the code of conduct go further, for example? There does remain some scope for tightening up and updating. A useful addition would be a clause dealing with panel surveys, which required the media to publish information about the size and bias of panel mortality, and the weighting procedure (if any) used as a corrective. A definition of 'sampling method' needs to be agreed upon: sometimes poll stories included details about the number of sampling points, or the design of the 'quota frame', sometimes not. They always should. And further thinking must be done about control over secondary reporting of polls. Even more important, the code of conduct needs to adapt to the different circumstances of television reporting, as TV companies increasingly commission polls. In the 1979 campaign television was considerably less dutiful than the press in reporting the technical details of fieldwork or providing the exact wording of questions. Relegating such details to the small print at the end of the newspaper story is no great sacrifice, broadcasting them in prime screen time however is quite another matter.

But flouting the code of conduct was not the main source of mis-reporting; indeed, there is a danger that by publishing the technical details of the poll, journalists will feel free to ignore the rules of proper interpretation in the rest of their story. Changes beyond a tinkering with the code of conduct are needed. One improvement would be the commissioning of more large-scale surveys (with larger samples and longer interviews), at the expense of the short 'quickie' which should be confined to eve-of-poll forecasting. This would allow for more refined analysis and for coverage extending beyond 'horse-race' commentary. A second area for improvement is prompted by the fact that, as this paper shows, the worst cases of misreporting tend to be committed by political correspondents of the popular press, who, with honourable exceptions, are rarely trained or expert in the reading of opinion polls. The delegation of poll stories to an in-house specialist who could accumulate expertise, based on the building up of a relationship with the client's polling company, would be a welcome change. In turn, the polling companies could do more in the way of training and education: the joint publication of a handbook on the writing up and interpretation of polls, for example; or a training conference just before the election campaign. And finally, there is no substitute for constant and critical public scrutiny of both the polls and the media, to which this chapter, and the book of which it is part, make a contribution.

Note: Chapter 10

Ivor Crewe is at the Department of Government, University of Essex and is Director of the Social Science Research Council Survey Archive.

11

Newspaper Coverage of the Polls

JOHN BARTER

The first point to make about newspaper coverage of the polls in the 1979 election is that there really was a lot of it. In the first two weeks of the campaign, no more than two days went by without the publication of a national poll. In the last two weeks, no more than a day went by without a poll being published. There were twenty-five national polls of voting intention and four *Sunday Times* panel polls, eight national polls in Scotland, polls in marginals, polls in key seats, polls of young mothers, polls of Liberal seats, polls of coloured voters and polls of new voters. This profusion of polls, listed in Table 10.1 of Ivor Crewe's paper in this volume (Chapter 10), certainly adds up to more polls and more newspaper coverage than at any previous election. Part of the reason for this may have been that newspapers had more money on this occasion and were prepared to put aside a bigger budget for polls. In addition, it may well have been that plans were rather better laid than is usually the case. Many people had planned on the assumption of an election in the autumn of 1978, and these plans may have been simply dredged up again when the election finally arrived.

The number of companies conducting polls notwithstanding, all the polls used quota samples at this election. Previously, polls had varied between quota and random samples. I think all the major pollsters now accept that time pressures mean that quota sampling is actually better than random sampling in a general election. There just isn't enough time to get a good contact rate on a random sample. Better to be up to date than to be what some would claim to be technically more correct.

In the event, the polls did fantastically well. Table 11.1 compares the final polls with the actual result, a comparison which shows just how well most of the polls performed. At NOP we felt fairly sore, because we were 1·6 per cent out on the Liberals, a result with which we would have been fairly happy had not everyone else been even closer. Much of the success of the polls in 1979 must be attributed to luck; we can never expect to be that much in agreement again.

Table 11.1 *Final Pre-Election Polls and the Election Result: Great Britain*

	Gallup	Marplan	NOP	MORI	Result
Fieldwork	April 30–May 1	May 1	May 1–2	May 2	
Sample size	2348	1973	1069	1089	
	%	%	%	%	%
Conservative	43.0	45.0	46.0	45.0	44.9
Labour	41.0	38.5	39.0	37.0	37.7
Liberal	13.5	13.5	12.5	15.0	14.1
Other	2.5	3.0	2.5	3.0	3.3
Conservative lead	2.0	6.5	7.0	8.0	7.2

Table 11.2 *Final Pre-Election Polls and the Election Result: Scotland*

	NOP	ORC	System 3	MORI	Result
Fieldwork	April 24–26	April 27–29	April 28–29	April 30–May 1	
Sample size	806	1016	1091	1025	
	%	%	%	%	%
Conservative	33.0	34.0	30.0	30.0	31.4
Labour	44.0	42.0	41.0	44.0	41.5
Liberal	6.0	8.0	11.0	6.0	8.7
SNP	16.0	15.0	17.0	18.0	17.3
Other	1.0	1.0	1.0	2.0	1.0
Conservative lead	– 11.0	– 8.0	– 11.0	– 14.0	– 10.1

Table 11.2 shows the equivalent comparison for the Scottish polls. Although the fieldwork for the Scottish polls did not continue as late as the Britain-wide polls, the Scottish surveys also came fairly close to the eventual result. A Labour lead of 8–14 per cent in the polls, compared to an actual Labour lead in Scotland of 10·1 per cent. One of the most interesting features of newspaper coverage of the polls in this election was the attention paid to the eight Scottish polls (three by System Three for the *Glasgow Herald*; two by ORC for the *Scotsman*; two by MORI for the *Daily Express*; and one by NOP for the *Daily Mail*). Now, it's fully understandable that the *Herald* and *Scotsman* would both want to do their own polls in Scotland. The same is true of the *Express* which is also very strong in Scotland. However, the *Mail*'s perception of the necessity for a Scottish poll resulted very much from its feeling that Scotland was a separate issue. There was an awareness of the complex electoral effects of the SNP slippage which

had been taking place over the preceding winter, and an awareness too that this slippage could play a significant part in determining the result across Britain as a whole.

The Scottish polls were of interest for a second reason. Generally speaking, when polls are published in an election campaign, the politicians of the losing parties will say all polls are nonsense, and anyway our own private polls show a very different picture. Now, that didn't happen very much in this campaign, except in Scotland where the SNP carried out its own poll reputedly showing that the party was going to hold all its own seats. That was, I think, the only example in this campaign of politicians saying polls are complete nonsense, and then proving themselves wrong!

The performance of the polls in this election may have been remarkably good, but the polls and the manner in which they were reported none the less caused some controversy in the media and elsewhere. In the remainder of this paper I examine the substance of those criticisms and develop some criticisms of my own of the way newspapers handled the polls.

Undoubtedly, the single most important cause of controversy was the series of four polls conducted by Research Services Ltd (RSL) for the *Observer*. With oil money to spend, the *Observer* had entered the polling stakes in a substantial way. RSL too had little recent experience of political polling, although it had conducted political surveys regularly when Mark Abrams was with them a decade earlier, and intermittently since then. RSL's polls appeared to show a very substantial Tory lead, considerably greater than the lead reported in the other polls. In his report on the first RSL poll in the *Observer* on 8 April Anthony King wrote that a Tory lead of 21 per cent 'scarcely four weeks before polling day, is staggering. It is the largest lead ever recorded for any political party during a General Election campaign since opinion polls began in Britain in 1939'. He did, however, go on to say in the third column that 'RSL's findings could be a fluke. Any single survey, however carefully carried out, is subject to random errors and bias'. Now to their credit RSL were themselves worried about the difference between its polls and the others. They called together a convention of pollsters on 26 April at which Bob Worcester of MORI and myself were present, together with Norman Webb from Gallup. RSL said to us: look, fellows, this is what we have been doing – can you think of anything which may be wrong with what we have been doing? We offered two main observations. First, RSL did not at that stage ask what we call an 'incliners' question. This question ('Which party are you most inclined to support?') is normally asked of those respondents who initially refuse to say what their voting intention is, or who alternatively say they don't know which party they are going to vote for. Long experience shows that this whittling down of the 'don't knows' produces results which are closer to the final result than the figures obtained from the first question alone. RSL did in fact include the incliners question in their very last poll, which showed a reduced Tory lead of 11·5 per cent. The second feature of RSL's polling which concerned us was that they applied a weighting based on past voting. RSL asked people how they voted in October 1974 and weighted the results so that the 1974 figures, as recalled by respondents, accurately reflected the actual result. The effect of this procedure was to reduce the Conservative lead somewhat, so we couldn't say this was the root of the problem. Nevertheless, weighting by past voting is not a practice of which most pollsters approve, since people's recollection of past voting is so poor.

Whatever the full explanation for RSL's difficulties, it would be wrong to suppose that the results of all the other polls were accepted without demur. My own company, NOP, conducted a poll for the *Daily Mail* on 29–30 April, a poll showing a Labour lead of 0·7 per cent. Since this was the only national poll in the whole campaign to show a Labour lead, it created considerable comment. In fact, nearly everybody said it was nonsense. My own feeling is that our poll may have exaggerated the true position but that Conservative strength probably did bottom out over that weekend only to revive again during the week of the election itself. Though no other polls were conducted at precisely the same time as ours, two adjacent polls showed the smallest Conservative lead of any campaign polls apart from ours. MORI's poll taken on 26 April for the *Daily Express* showed a reduced Tory lead of 3 per cent, while Gallup's poll conducted for the *Daily Telegraph* on 30 April–1 May showed a Tory lead of 2·5 per cent, also down from Gallup's poll the week before. Perhaps the Labour Party never was actually in the lead but certainly the Tory margin became very slim at that point in the campaign.

Press coverage of the polls in 1979 included a good deal of sensible comment on how to read the polls and how to avoid some of the more common errors of interpretation. None the less, there are four specific points arising from the way polls were presented in the press to which attention should be drawn, for each point offers a lesson from which I hope future press coverage of the polls can learn.

The first point concerns a poll of black voters which appeared in the *Express* on 9 April. This survey purported to show a substantial drop in Labour's support among black immigrants in eight British cities. Although the *Express* had a contractual relationship with MORI, this poll was actually published without Bob Worcester knowing anything about it whatsoever. The poll was produced by one Sultan Mahmood, a freelance journalist of whom I had not previously heard. He used a collection of immigrant researchers to conduct the poll. The report states the sample size but says nothing at all about how the sample was drawn or when the interviews were conducted. I'm none too happy about some of the questions either. One question, for example, was 'Are the present laws sufficient to prevent racial incitement?' Now this question is not posed in a very sensible way, and I'm fairly certain that understanding of the term 'racial incitement' would be substantially less than 100 per cent. Another even stranger question was 'Will you live in Great Britain for ever?' Those of us who are regularly involved in polling ought to be wary of claiming a monopoly of the market but I feel nevertheless that newspapers ought to be very careful about using polls with a background that is difficult to authenticate.

'Polls of polls' are my second area of comment. A poll of polls consists simply of sticking the results of the latest polls together, weighting them by sample size and arriving at a single set of results. They were used quite extensively in the 1979 election. Again, I'm none too happy with this procedure. The best thing to do, in my opinion, is to report the most up-to-date poll and say what the previous results were. This was the method followed by *The Economist* in its sensible secondary report, 'Is the gap closing?', on 28 April. It is not a good idea to put together the results of different polls, even if they are conducted reasonably closely together. And the consequence of weighting by sample size is simply that if the biggest one happens to be wrong, the overall results are less accurate than if a weighting had not been applied.

Translating poll results into seat projections, my third criticism of the media's poll coverage, is a dangerous game which journalists have been playing for a long time with distinctly variable results. In the 1979 election *Weekend World* used its surveys in 100 marginal constituencies to make predictions about the likely distribution of seats in Parliament. 'Tories to win with overall majority of 60' was the headline of a report released by *Weekend World* on 22 April, eleven days before the election itself. Most pollsters would I think agree that it is not a good use of polls to translate vote intentions into seats, particularly when the election is still some way off. To be fair, most of the newspapers which regularly publish polls have learned to be more cautious on this point than they used to be.

Finally, in this series of criticisms, an additional comment on the treatment of 'don't knows' in voting surveys. Like RSL, Marplan also did not ask the 'incliners' question in all of its polls: '22 per cent don't know' was the resulting headline in the *Sun* over its report of a Marplan poll on 20 April. This was followed on 23 April by another report sub-headed '3 million don't knows hold key to poll'. Now, I don't think the 22 per cent who say they don't know which party they will vote for is necessarily an accurate reflection of the true situation. People may be slightly hesitant and may differ in the intensity of their preference, but I don't think that many people really 'don't know'.

Having ventured my own criticisms of newspaper coverage of the polls, I will now change tack and conclude by defending the press against some prevalent but none the less unjustified criticisms of its poll coverage. One common criticism, at this and preceding elections, is that there is too much concentration on voting intentions. Now, I just don't accept this. It's what the voters are interested in; it's what the newspapers are interested in. It sets the campaign in context and I don't think this emphasis is a bad use of polls, provided other material is supplied by the polling company – and other material is usually supplied though it is often not used. The fact that there are so many voting surveys is actually very comforting, since the odd 'rogue' poll becomes much easier to identify even though it may still be widely reported. And in view of Ivor Crewe's criticisms of the use of polls by the media elsewhere in this book, it is worth mentioning here the four-wave *Sunday Times*/MORI panel study, written up by Peter Kellner in the *New Statesman*. Here was a study which was *not* set up to measure voting intentions but which was intended to see how and why people changed their intentions during the campaign. This study did, I think, provide some of the more detailed analysis of the electorate's attitude and behaviour which Ivor Crewe complains did not exist.

Before the election, many people suggested that the marginal constituencies were the real battleground of the election. Since those constituencies were the only ones that really mattered, the argument ran, why not restrict all polling to them? This view is superficially attractive but, I think, mistaken none the less. The problem with polls in the marginals is that they will only be more accurate than a national poll if the swing is homogeneous within the marginals – and we know this assumption is increasingly false. The results of the 1979 election have, in fact, confirmed my preference for national polls over both polls in the marginals and other types of special polls.

Note: Chapter 11

John Barter is Managing Director of National Opinion Polls (NOP) and Chairman of the Market Research Society.

12

ITN's Use of Opinion Polls

PAUL McKEE

News at Ten featured an opinion poll story on 22 of the 35 days between the defeat of the government and polling day. In most such stories we gave the results of national opinion polls scheduled for appearance in a newspaper the following morning. The extent of our poll coverage increased slightly compared with 1974, reflecting no doubt the increase in 1979 in the number of polls commissioned. In this paper I summarise ITN's approach to poll material of this kind, covering in turn (1) the house-rules we have developed for reporting polls; (2) the reasoning behind our decision not to commission voting-intention polls ourselves apart from our on-the-day poll; (3) our use of a special poll to help guide ITN's own election coverage during the campaign; and (4) the 'on-the-day poll' reported on election night itself.

House-Rules

One can confidently predict that at some point in every election campaign a letter will appear in one of the quality papers attacking the use of polling information by the media. I defend our use of polls against such attacks partly by saying that if poll findings were not made public in this fashion, they would just be leaked into the public domain in a selected and distorted way. In addition, however, I feel that the opinions of 1,000 or so people selected in a responsible and moderately scientific way are more representative than the opinions of any one individual, no matter how well informed that individual may be. So it is, I think, reasonable to regard polling information as at least potentially newsworthy.

However, we have in ITN developed a number of house-rules which we apply to polling information. The first of these is that we always try to put poll data in the context of other important events. In other words, we will never lead a bulletin on a poll story. This is a practice we have followed consistently over the last few elections.

The second house-rule relates to the problem of balance in our election coverage. How does one go about providing balance in one's coverage of polls? One method we adopt is to demonstrate by covering all the major national polls that poll results are likely to vary. Another method is to cover not only the 'horse-race' element in the polls, but also to blend in to our coverage other information from the polls – on leadership ratings, on key issues, on marginal polls and on regional polls. These approaches give us an element of balance within our overall coverage of the polls.

The third house-rule is to source the poll. Pressure on television time is so acute that we can only give a relatively short amount of time to any particular poll. It is, therefore, important to source the poll, so that viewers have ready access to further information.

The fourth and, in a sense, the most obvious house-rule is that we only feature polls which we expect to prove reliable. Establishing the likely reliability of a poll is no problem with reputable organisations from whom technical details of the poll are readily available, but there are always one or two less well-known organisations which come into the polling business, usually at a regional or constituency level, at election time. One has to keep a watchful eye on these organisations and perhaps, press them for further details before deciding whether or not to run their results. In 1979 we spiked one national poll plus a couple of regional polls for which technical details weren't available or which had results which simply didn't look right. There were also a number of constituency polls which weren't important enough to feature or which just didn't hang together with the rest of the bulletin. But the reliability of national polls is usually fairly easy to check.

We are sometimes criticised for failing to give in our bulletins the technical details of the polls which we report – details of sample size, number of sampling points, and so on. Although pressure on time precludes us from providing this information, our house-rules have been designed to minimise the resulting problem. We do source the poll, so that people can readily obtain the technical information for themselves, and we do try to screen out unreliable polls altogether. In addition, we hope that the very fact that we have decided to carry a poll indicates to the viewer that the poll is likely to prove reliable.

Why We Don't Commission Voting Surveys during Campaigns

Although ITN is an organisation which is prepared to commission polls, we adopt a deliberate policy of not commissioning voting-intention polls during election campaigns, with the exception of the on-the-day poll I discuss below. Since I've already argued that an election campaign is the precise period when voting surveys are most newsworthy, it is worthwhile explaining the reasoning behind this self-denying ordinance.

We first adopted the policy in the 1960s, when we were concerned about just how advanced the art or science of opinion polling actually was. We recognised that opinion polling was certainly not an exact science, and we were concerned about the effect on us of being known as an organisation which had commissioned a 'rogue' poll. Underlying this concern was an awareness of our statutory obligation to be fair and impartial. The need to be scrupulously impartial is a fundamental operating rule which runs through many decision-making procedures in any broadcasting organisation in Britain. In these circumstances we felt then (and to some extent we still take this view today) that the risk of a 'rogue' poll is too great to warrant ITN commissioning its own voting surveys during election campaigns. In addition, there would be a natural tendency for us to feature our own polls in a slightly heavier and stronger way than other polls of equal repute.

These historical reasons have to some extent been supplanted by a more recent concern. If we were to commission our own poll, we would feel obliged to give it more time on the bulletin than we would to a report of someone else's poll. Even though copies of the poll would be available to people who wrote in, the prime source of information would be the broadcast itself. Hence, we would need to provide more technical information than it would be possible to squeeze into the strictly limited amount of space which is available for a report on any single poll, no matter how important.

Using Polls to Influence Campaign Coverage

Although we did not commission any polls of voting intentions before election day itself, we did not dispense with surveys altogether. Early on in the campaign, we commissioned a survey to find out what issues the electorate thought television should concentrate on during the campaign. The findings of this survey proved to be a significant influence on our coverage.

One modest initiative we took during the campaign was to include in our coverage a comparison of the parties' positions on various issues. This was something that had not been previously attempted in a news context by ourselves or the BBC. The exercise was fraught with difficulties, not the least of which was the likelihood of the parties objecting that we had misrepresented their positions. But the first problem we faced was deciding on which issues to focus this comparison. There was already substantial polling information available on what people thought were, or ought to be, the most important issues in the campaign. But we felt it worth while asking the question in a slightly different way and seeing which issues people would be most interested in seeing discussed on television. Not surprisingly, the five issues that came out top in our poll were also top of the other polls conducted that week by Marplan, MORI and RSL. Four of the five issues also appeared in NOP's top five issues of the week. We felt, none the less, that our own findings gave us a more solid underpinning on which to base our selection of issues. During the campaign, we did produce reports on these issues to a standard format, with a brief introduction to the problem followed by a comparison of the parties' positions. We tried to make these often abstract problems appear more interesting by introducing them in most cases with a cartoon.

In addition to asking our respondents *which* issues should be covered on television, we also asked *how* the campaign could best be covered. We wanted to find out which of several ways of covering an election on television was most attractive to people. We did not slavishly follow the results, but again the results did have some impact on the nature of our coverage. At the top of the list came phone-in programmes, with politicians answering viewers' questions, and a televised debate between the leaders of the two main parties. Neither of these ideas was of much practical value for us. Phone-in sessions are difficult to incorporate within a news bulletin, and the idea of a televised debate had already been rejected by Mrs Thatcher. The second level contained a series of items closely grouped in popularity: comparison of policies on various issues; studio discussions between politicians; and interviews with party leaders. The third level contained the least-popular forms of coverage: party political broadcasts; film extracts of politicians' speeches; reports from different regions of the country; reports from individual constituencies; reports of opinion polls; and reports of the parties' daily press conferences. There are two interpretations one can place on this long list of relatively unpopular items. One is that people just don't like coverage of these items and that they should, therefore, be dropped. The other is that we should pull our socks up and make our presentation in these areas more attractive and interesting. Which of these interpretations is correct, I just don't know. It remains to be seen what trends are revealed by subsequent surveys of this kind.

It was clear from these results that there was room for improvement in the appeal of our opinion-poll presentations. How, then, did we go about trying to improve our poll coverage? One way was by deliberately setting out in our daily reporting of opinion polls to put the information in a clear, standard framework. The following extract from *News at Ten* on 10 April is a typical example:

The Conservatives are still leading Labour by ten points in the MORI poll to be published in tomorrow's *Daily Express*. That's three points down compared to the last MORI poll. The Conservatives are given 49 per cent, Labour 39 per cent, Liberals 10 per cent, others 2 per cent. But Mr Callaghan has moved further ahead of Mrs Thatcher as the better Prime Minister. The poll? Mr Callaghan, up from 42 per cent to 47 per cent; Mrs Thatcher much the same, 40 per cent down to 39 per cent; don't know, 14 per cent. And should Mrs Thatcher have debated with Mr Callaghan on television? The answer is even: should have accepted, 47 per cent; should not, 45 per cent; don't know, 8 per cent.

The basic voting-intention figures are put in the context of previous surveys and a brief reference to levels and trends in leadership ratings is followed by the results of a question on a televised debate between the party leaders, an issue which was particularly current at that point in the campaign.

Another initiative we took in our poll coverage was to bring together the week's polls on our Sunday transmission. This allowed us to demonstrate trends and to highlight the results of marginal polls and Scottish surveys, thus pointing to the possibility of regional divergence from national figures. On the last Sunday of the campaign, for example, we showed the decline in the Tory lead and the growing strength of the Liberals. So the Sunday broadcast was used to put the polls into perspective and point out some of their implications. We did not, however, fall into the trap mentioned by John Barter (NOP) of mechanically translating poll results into seat projections. There is nothing which irritates me more than an opinion poll being converted by the simplest of methods into a seat projection. We did talk about the lead in the opinion polls which the Conservatives needed to obtain an overall majority but that was all.

People are keen to tell you in casual conversation about opinion polls that they have never been interviewed; that their spouse has never been interviewed; that none of their friends has ever been interviewed; and that neither they, nor their spouse nor any of their friends, even know anyone who has ever been interviewed. In the light of this attitude, we thought it might be useful to include in our coverage a background report on opinion polls, showing how the pollsters go about their job. In the final week of the campaign, therefore, Bob Hargreaves spent some time with Gallup, watching an interviewer at work. This is the text of his report shown on *News at Ten*:

Once every week during the campaign a small army of Gallup

pollsters takes to the streets in search of opinions. Veronica Klein is one of them. Her task today? To investigate in depth the intentions of ten voters in the Wycombe constituency of Buckinghamshire.

Gallup Interviewer:	'Who would make the better Prime Minister – Mr Callaghan, Mrs Thatcher, or Mr Steel?'
First Respondent:	'Mr Steel, I think.'

Selecting people to interview in an opinion poll is not as random as it appears. Veronica's ten voters have to be a statistically defined cross section. So many unemployed; so many self-employed; so many men and so many women; so many who live in council houses and so many who own their own homes; so many young and so many old.

Interviewer:	'Leaving on one side your own hopes, which party do you think will in fact win the general election?'
Second Respondent:	'Well, I hope it will be Labour. I'm hoping.'
Interviewer:	'Who do you think will win?'
Second Respondent:	'Well, I think it will be Labour.'
Reporter:	'Why did you choose to interview that particular chap?'
Interviewer:	'Well, first, because he was a captive audience. He didn't look like he could run away too fast, probably a pensioner. I could tell his age, his socioeconomic grouping and whether he was working or not just looking at him.'

One of the main hazards the pollsters face is the brush-off. Polite . . .

Interviewer:	'May I interview you?'
First Non-Respondent:	'I would rather you didn't, thank you.'

or not so polite . . .

Interviewer:	'Morning. I'm doing a survey for Gallup Poll for the general election.'
Second Non-Respondent:	'Not today, you're not.'

Eventually, Veronica finds a willing victim with the right profile.

Third
Respondent: 'I used to be a socialist. I'm speaking as someone who was brought up with socialism but I'm thoroughly disillusioned.'

Each subject has been carefully selected – and needs to be, since each interview represents the intentions of over 20,000 other voters.

Interviewer: 'If your vote decided whether we had a Labour government under Mr Callaghan or a Conservative government under Mrs Thatcher, which would you choose?'
Fourth
Respondent: 'I don't prefer the lady. I prefer a man.'

Interviewing is surprisingly detailed: about forty questions to each person who agrees to answer them not only about their vote, but about themselves.

Interviewer: 'Do you belong to a trade union?'
Fourth
Respondent: 'I classify myself as middle-class now, because I've got nearly what I want.'

It's taken Veronica about two hours to find her ten voters. Now, her answers are sent back to be entered in Gallup's election computer. Back in London the ten questionnaires filled out by Veronica Klein and 200 other interviewers are being punched out on to card indices, and from here they will be fed into Gallup's central computer for analysis of the outcome of the poll. 2,000 voters have been questioned for the poll spread evenly across the 200 constituencies. Gallup claim their methods are accurate to about 3 per cent. We'll only know whether they are right or wrong on election night. But polls, often derided, have become as central a part of our campaigning as hecklers at meetings or canvassers on the doorstep. (Robert Hargreaves, *News at Ten*, with the Gallup pollsters)

On-the-Day Poll

In terms of polls that we commission ourselves, the majority of our effort and money goes into an on-the-day poll which we conduct with voters as they are emerging from polling stations up and down the country. This is a technique which we have developed over the last few years and which we have now applied to three general elections, the Common Market referendum, the two devolution referendums and ten or so by-elections. We have developed the technique to the point where we can now get a fairly complicated questionnaire answered, even if it is raining or snowing. So we can now get not only a prediction of the result, but also an analysis of why people voted the way they did.

The only occasion on which the use of this technique led us to pick the wrong winner was Austin Mitchell's by-election at Grimsby. We were only polling at four of the forty-three polling stations on that occasion and it transpired that the interviewers at two of these stations were only interviewing half the people they should have been. The figures were internally consistent; it simply looked as though turnout was down, when in fact turnout went up substantially. But of the many hundreds of polling stations at which we have conducted on-the-day polls, these are the only two where we have had difficulties with interviewers. (We sent a suitable letter of apology to Austin afterwards.)

Table 12.1 *ITN's Election-Night Forecast and the Election Result*

	Forecast	Result	Difference
Conservative	349	339	+ 10
Labour	257	269	− 12
Liberal	12	11	+ 1
SNP	2	2	0
Other	15	14	+ 1
Conservative overall majority	63	43	+ 20

The accuracy of our on-the-day poll in 1979 can be gauged from Table 12.1. We were ten seats out on the Conservatives, twelve out on Labour and one out on the Liberals. Although we got the SNP figure right in aggregate, we predicted that they would hold on to the Western Isles and Argyll, when in fact they lost in Argyll but held on to Dundee East. Overall, these results were not as good as October 1974, when we were at most six seats out on any single party. But we were right in headline terms: we said that the Conservatives would win with a significant working majority; that the SNP would be decimated; and that the Liberals would stay more or less the same. That, I think, was a good starting-point for the election-night programme.

We are, of course, frequently criticised for overdoing the 'horse-race' element in the election by conducting these same-day polls. Why not, the argument runs, wait until the next day when all the results will be known anyway? I would defend our use of on-the-day polls by saying that the result is what people are sitting at home waiting for. The on-the-day poll gives us a good starting-point; it gives us an opportunity to say to our viewers: 'this is what we *think* is going to happen but now let's wait and see what actually *does* happen. Let's open a good bottle or have a cup of tea.'

Note: Chapter 12

Paul McKee is at Independent Television News.

13
Political Parties and Private Polls

DENNIS KAVANAGH

Private polls for the Conservative and Labour parties have become almost as much a part of the election scene as are the public polls. Over the years British parties have become more concerned about influencing voters and exploiting social science and commercial techniques to this end. Opinion polls seem to be an inevitable part of the move towards more elaborate, sophisticated and expensive efforts in publicity and communication.[1] Yet one says 'almost' because influential figures in both parties still question whether private polls give value for money.

A 'private' poll may conjure up visions of some ultra-sensitive information discovered by arcane techniques and potentially capable of swinging an election. In fact, shrewd strategists in one party can usually guess what questions the rival party will be asking and what they will find. A good deal of general information is already available in the published polls on which the private pollster and parties draw.

The purpose of this paper is to try to shed light on this private world by studying the role of private polls prior to 1979, their use in the 1979 election and, finally, by assessing their general import in British politics.

The two main parties in Britain have used the private polls for three broad types of operations. (1) They have used panels of voters to collect baseline data and formulate *long-term* strategy, with particular groups of voters being re-interviewed between and during elections. (2) During the elections 'quickie' surveys are conducted on reactions to particular issues, themes, personalities and broadcasts. A small group (usually 500–700 people) is interviewed, so that issues and images can be 'tracked'. These deal with *short-term* tactics. Speed is essential here; in a developing campaign situation information can be out of date in twenty-four hours. Finally, there are *medium-term* surveys, which deal with reactions to by-elections, slogans and manifesto issues, and generally assess the impact of a party's efforts in political communications.

For an illustration of the varied uses of private polls one may point to the following areas.

(a) *Image-building*: in 1966 the private polls showed that the Conservatives were regarded as old-fashioned and out of touch, following their years in office over 1951–64. These findings reinforced the decision to concentrate publicity on the party's new policies and leaders. After February 1974, ORC's findings on the public dislike of adversary aspects of party politics and one-party government, and the potential for Liberal support, were important in developing the 'national unity' package for the October election.

(b) *Policy*: formally, the policy-making exercise in both parties is separate from the publicity one and polls are used for the presentation and emphasis not the formulation of policy. But the distinction is not a hard-and-fast one and assessments of public opinion do play a part in affecting policy positions. It is, however, difficult to pin down cases of the private polls actually influencing the content of policy. The difficulty in discerning the influence is that it is probably wise for a pollster, who wishes to have a long-term relationship with a party, not to emphasise his influence on politicians. The latter also have an interest in not publicising the relationship. However, Humphrey Taylor's private polls certainly contributed to the Conservatives boosting old-age pensions and introducing pensions for the over-80s after 1970, promoting the sale of council houses to tenants and accepting comprehensive education despite the opposition of many party activists. In the Labour party the polls were important in encouraging leaders to soft-pedal nationalisation in 1964 and 1966 and press devolution for Scotland in October 1974.

(c) *Tracking issues*: both parties now regularly monitor the changing salience of issues and themes in the election; they also ask such questions as 'Which party is best at handling . . .?' for each issue, with the result that they divide the election agenda into 'our' issues and 'theirs'. The shift in ground in February 1974 from the 'who governs' issues to prices was favourable to Labour and presaged the movement in votes.[2] In 1979 'taxation' and 'law and order' were generally regarded as strong Conservative issues. The polls also discern 'sleeper' issues by asking voters which issues they think *should* be important, as opposed to those which *are*.

(d) *Identification* (and approval) of campaign themes, slogans and manifesto proposals: the Conservatives have tended to do this type of research more regularly than Labour, perhaps because they poll more continuously. For the last two elections, the Conservative private polls have tried to measure the impact of the party's advertising and, in 1979, they tested reactions to Labour's manifesto.

(e) *Target voters*: surveys are important in identifying relevant features of the targets of campaign broadcasts and advertising. Before 1964, the parties had tended to focus their propaganda on their 'solid' voters and not systematically sought information about the concerns of different groups of voters. Surveys were important in showing how volatile many voters were and the large number who were potentially detachable from the two main parties. In the 1964 election Mark Abrams described the target voters as 'uncommitted voters in uncommitted constituencies'.[3]

The parties now use polls to divide the electorate, broadly, into 'ours', 'theirs' and 'uncertain'. Both generally agree on the criteria to identify potential 'floating' voters – those one party may lose or gain and these tend to be less interested, informed and exposed to politics than the more partisan. In the 1974 elections both ORC and MORI used more detailed analyses of voter panels to identify potential converts and the issues which appeal to them. Over the years, the identification of the target voter with a relatively non-partisan voter has encouraged a focus on bread-and-butter issues and a more pragmatic outlook. Labour has weaned itself from its cloth-cap image and the Conservatives have tried to lose their suburban, pin-stripe image.

(*f*) *Election timing*: in January 1974 ORC polled on attitudes to the miners' strike and advised an early election if the Tories were to have a good chance of winning. The advice was ignored. In summer 1978 MORI's depressing report of its marginal seats survey helped dissuade Mr Callaghan from going to the country.

The 1979 Election

LABOUR

In the first year or two after 1974 the Labour Party, for financial and other reasons, did not conduct any polls, although Mr Wilson arranged for the funding of private MORI research during the Common Market referendum in 1975. Apart from a few by-election studies, the Labour party only resumed polling on a substantial scale in 1978, after the NEC had voted £50,000 for such work on 20 February by 11 votes to 7. A committee of sympathetic academics continued to provide independent advice on Mr Worcester's polling strategy (rejecting some of his proposals), and in April Ivor Crewe of Essex University made a presentation of his British Election Study findings to the Campaign Committee. A large-scale study in Scotland showed that devolution was a low priority among Scottish electors, but the impact of its findings was diminished by the fact that the Labour victories in the Garscadden and Hamilton by-elections occurred while the survey was being processed. A more influential study of marginal seats was also initiated. It was a panel study with something under 1,000 respondents in seventy-one seats; they were interviewed first in April 1978, then in August and then again in January 1979.

The first survey was particularly gloomy, suggesting that Labour was faring even worse in marginal seats than in the country as a whole. Some of the findings were leaked (by a Labour MP) to the press in July and certainly influenced Mr Callaghan during his August meditations on whether to call an autumn election Mr Callaghan took the results to his Sussex farm and, as he compared its findings with the latest *Times Guide to the House of Commons*, he could not see where likely Labour gains would come from. The August survey was also depressing but, contrary to rumour, Mr Callaghan did not have access to the findings at the time of his final decision in early September. The surveys carried bad news not only on voting intentions, but on attitudes to issues. On the problems to which voters gave most priority – unemployment, law and order and inflation – Labour trailed the Conservatives. The only comfort was that Mr Callaghan was regarded a better Prime Minister than Mrs Thatcher would be.

When the election came, MORI was authorised to produce regular private polls, though on a more limited scale than hitherto. There was the inevitable debate on the NEC as to whether the party needed the polls and, if so, should spend £48,000 on them. But Mr Callaghan's wish prevailed. During 7–30 April there were ten 'quickie' polls in contrast to seventeen during the shorter campaign of October 1974. A quota sample of 720 electors, ten from each of seventy-two marginal seats, were asked a dozen or so questions. The operation was similar to that of previous elections. The results of the fieldwork were phoned in by 6.30 p.m. and a report was prepared by Bob Worcester. If there was anything startling, he would phone Mr Callaghan and Mr Hayward that night. The figures, together with a photocopied handwritten report, were sent to Number 10 for Mr Callaghan's 7.30 breakfast meeting with his aides. He also presented his findings to the heads of departments meeting and the Campaign Committee. He appended to his survey reports a summary of the main findings of his own and other public polls.

The story his polls had to tell was of an advance on all fronts – but one that was too slow to make up for the initial deficit. Even at the end of the campaign, the Conservatives were seen as having the better policies on all the main issues except the handling of strikes and the health service. On taxes and on law and order Labour was over 30 per cent behind. Labour had lost ground among young housewives in the C_2 group and many potential Labour voters were not very concerned about the election. The most consoling findings were that Labour was seen as having the better leaders, that Labour's party political broadcasts were more appreciated, and that slightly more blame was attributed to the Conservatives for making the election a slanging match and making promises which the country could not afford. The MORI polls showed areas in which Labour policies were popular but not understood by the public, for example, on free TV licences for pensioners, and pledges to offer the unemployed a job or retraining. They also suggested a greater emphasis on the Common Market and the health service.

On 26 April he wrote: 'The Party must, in the last few days, give Labour supporters a belief that the election does matter and that the Labour Party is a party of compassion and one that keeps its promises.' His final report on 30 April contained what he termed 'better news':

> The public now thinks that prices would go up faster under the Tories, as would strikes *and* unemployment. They still believe, however, that the average person's take-home pay would be higher under the Conservatives.

CONSERVATIVES

During the parliament the Conservatives spent more money and time on polls than Labour; they were more consistent in sponsoring them and more sophisticated in making use of them, particularly in the years before the election. Detailed planning of the party's polling programme for the election itself began in early 1978, in anticipation of an autumn general election. Three major surveys were conducted over the summer and the findings, though reporting Labour's recovery,were heartening for the Conservatives. A clear majority of voters were pessimistic about the country's economic future and Labour was still tinged with the image of 'extremism'. Above all, the surveys showed the fragility of Labour's recovery. Whereas three-quarters of 'strong' and 'weak' Conservatives thought their party would win a general election, only 60 per cent of 'strong' Labour and 32 per cent of 'weak' Labour supporters were confident about their party's prospects. Another heartening finding was on preferences for alternative election outcomes; 32 per cent wanted a clear Conservative victory, 28 per cent a coalition of the parties and only 22 per cent a clear Labour victory.

During the election the findings of the ORC polls were much more widely disseminated through the party hierarchy than under the old regime (but with notably few leaks). Up to fifty copies of the findings were quickly circulated with a brief commentary on the key points by Keith Britto of the Research Department, who worked full-time on the polls. Mr Hanvey, unlike Mr Worcester, did not make a formal presentation of his findings to a campaign committee. A regular report on the findings of the published polls was also produced. In contrast to Mr Worcester's written comments on his reports, Mr Britto's were mere factual recapitulations of the main findings and rarely made suggestions for campaign tactics.

During the election the Conservatives, like Labour, abandoned the daily polls of 1974. Their major effort went into four 'state of battle' surveys (based on weekend interviews with voters in England and Wales), ready on each Monday from 3 April, and on five 'quickie' surveys each mid-week (a sixth was added on 28 April). They also conducted a survey after each party election broadcast (except the last two Liberal ones). These were supplemented by special surveys of Liberals in two types of English constituencies – strong Liberal seats and Conservative–Labour marginals – and in Scottish seats.

The polls were rather longer and more wide-ranging than Labour's and on the whole their readers must have found them highly encouraging, including the overwhelming majority (65–25 per cent) recorded on 23 April for 'a completely new approach' with twice as many thinking the Conservatives would provide it (35 per cent Conservatives to 19 per cent Labour). On the other hand, a really worrying finding in the polls was the continued evidence of the Liberals' potential. By 15 April 47 per cent of the electorate, including well over one-third of Conservative and Labour supporters, agreed with the statement 'It's about time we gave the Liberals a chance'. The polls did give early warning that the Conservatives were not doing well among pensioners (concerned about higher indirect taxes) and led to specific efforts to reassure them. Attitudes on the tax issue were ambiguous; support for a reduction in direct taxation, but concern about cuts in public services and higher direct taxes. 'Handle with care' was the general message, as Labour's attacks gradually blunted the Conservative appeal.

Politicians are, as a rule, more inclined to heed polls when their import justifies the current strategy. The polls (public and private) provide only one sort of evidence, and it has to be set against reports from the constituencies and the leadership's own sense of the electoral mood. Mrs Thatcher has a combative side and there were complaints from the grass roots that the party was conducting too 'soft' a campaign. But the poll findings encouraged those campaign advisers who resisted pressure for a bold counterattack on Labour. ORC reported that voters did not like an adversarial approach, wanted to hear about positive policies and that the party was likely to lose from a more heated campaign. A number of critics took a 'so what?' stance towards some of the findings. They were not clear about the consequences of the survey findings for policy and presentation, and would have welcomed more explicit political advice.

Reading through the poll reports for the two parties, however, it is hard to see what important action points could have flowed from them in what was a rather sluggish campaign. The issues that mattered to the electorate did not change much, and the private findings did not conflict with what the public-opinion polls were saying. When little is stirring the electorate, the great value of up-to-date private polls is that they can justify the leadership in staying firmly on course, unpanicked by its excitable supporters. On the occasions when there is a change in mood or the emergence of a new issue in mid-campaign a daily poll can give some measure of scale to a phenomenon that would not in any case go unnoticed. In 1979 the situation did not arise.

Conclusion

What conclusions may we draw about the political role of the private polling in the light of the 1979 election? There were many similarities in the remit of the two pollsters; they used the same techniques, conducted national, local and regional surveys; and their findings on issues, personalities, reactions to broadcasts, and their potential 'soft' centres of support in the electorate (both were aware of the volatility of C_2 housewives), and the issues and themes to mobilise their strong supporters, hardly differed from each other or those of the public polls. But the Conservative machine appears to have thought more carefully about the purposes of the polls, polled more continuously, made more use of surveys in the run-up to the election, and better integrated the findings into their publicity effort. By contrast, MORI was given a budget and that (after some opposition by the NEC) only when the campaign was under way; little advance or continuous research was done: the scale of polling was reduced compared to 1974; and Mr Worcester was not closely involved with the advertising team before or during the campaign. Labour's advertising team made little use of his material; they were interested in depth studies more than in trend data. With the growing importance of television as the major source of communication for most voters, and the role of the party leader as the bearer of the party's message on and off television, the pollster's influence depends, ultimately, on his access to the leader or the people around him. In that regard, ORC had an advantage over MORI in 1979.

The different party structures are important in explaining the contrast. The ORC pollster formally reports to the party chairman who is in charge of Central Office and is directly appointed by the party leader. This potential concentration of decision-making simplifies communication within the party. MORI formally reports to Labour's General Secretary who is appointed by and responsible to the NEC. In recent years a majority on this body has been at odds with the parliamentary leadership. For the past twenty-five years successive party leaders have been sympathetic to the polling exercise, while many on the NEC have been opposed. Yet regardless of the party leader's (or Prime Minister's) wishes, it is up to the NEC to commission polls and authorise the release of funds. Because of the organisational complexity and policy divisions in the party, a Labour pollster can and does find himself exposed to conflicting demands.[4]

This is not to say that the differences between the two parties are permanent – witness the Labour effort in 1962–4 – but that these tendencies appear to be implicit in the party structures. Another way of describing the contrast is to note that Labour leaders since 1960 have used polls to communicate with the electorate, while many members of the NEC are more oriented to 'the party' or Conference which elects them. On the other hand, Conservative leaders, with the possible exception of Mr Heath, have been less interested in the polls, while the party organisation has become more oriented to the electorate than the NEC.

It is worth reflecting on the lack of clear guidelines for relations between the pollster and the party. The pollster is an outsider compared to other members of the regular party machine. He is recruited for his expertise in a particular area – monitoring and interpreting public opinion – and is employed on a contractual basis. This reflects the strengths and limits of his position. As a general rule the more he adheres to a limited 'expert' role, the less political influence he is likely to have. But the more he moves to offering policy recommendations, the more likely his clients are to question both his judgement and his expertise.

The pollster's problem, however, is that different people have different, even conflicting, expectations of what he can and should do. In both parties some campaigners want explicit guidance about the implications of data that they did not find interesting in itself, while others – particularly in the Labour party – would deeply resent such a step. To quote Bob Worcester:

> I characterise the responsibility I have as one of bringing witness to the ripples, the waves and the tides. If the Labour Party leadership wants to swim against the tide of public opinion that is their responsibility. I see my role as telling them which way the tide is running and how strongly, and then I stop. I would find it very

difficult to be both an objective analyst of public opinion and party strategist and political adviser.[5]

The pollster takes risks in reporting or commenting, even implicitly, on issues which are the subject of intra-party tensions. Most politicians are jealous of their own sphere of competence, *vis-à-vis* pollsters, publicists and the media; they also know that poll data may be employed by their opponents to undermine their standing nationally and in the party. Where a pollster crosses the demarcation line and is accepted, it is usually because he has developed a reputation for good political judgement. Mark Abrams, by 1964, and Humphrey Taylor, during 1965–75, were closely involved with their parties' plans. In both cases, personal relations were important. Yet too close an identification with a leader's point of view in a divided party may weaken the pollster's position, if there is a change of policy or leadership in the party.

A Labour pollster faces the additional hazards of coping with the party factions and both Abrams and Worcester have encountered opposition. Worcester's findings (reported in public polls also) inevitably became a weapon in the bitter left vs right disputes on the NEC and in the Campaign Committee. The findings about the public hostility to the trade unions and to many of the personalities and policies associated with the party's left wing aroused bitter antagonism. In 1973 he was instructed by Mr Benn to discontinue research into the popularity of politicians, though Mr Wilson instructed him to continue with this research, and in 1974 to stop making editorial comments in his *Public Opinion Digest*.

A number of factors affect the influence of the private pollster. The 1979 experience again supports the view that the closeness of a pollster to the party's strategic thinking varies with the party's position in government or opposition. Ministers are busy and tend to be more concerned to implement and justify existing programmes than to test new policies for their electoral popularity. The party machine – to whom the pollster reports – also tends to take a back seat when the party is in government. Of course, other factors affect the closeness of the relationship but it is interesting that the Conservatives were less interested in polling during 1970–74, and mounted their most ambitious survey programmes in the three periods of opposition since 1966. Labour's major use of polls have been the opposition periods 1962–4 and 1972–4, with little being done for the 1966 and 1970 elections and only a modest amount in 1979.

One can certainly point to cases where, over the years, the private polls have been influential in affecting the balance of a decision. But it is possible to exaggerate their actual and potential influence. To have impact, the message of the polls usually has to be consistent with other cues. British parties are programmatic; they have their own interests, traditions and values to protect. Politicians have other sources of information. In the course of many interviews with politicians and officials it is very rare that they refer spontaneously to the polls.

Understanding of the polls among politicians and officials is variable. Some still demand, literally, 'good news', get excited over a small and statistically insignificant shift of opinion, or judge the pollster crudely on the basis of his prediction.[6] However unfairly, the private polls, like the party machine and political leadership, become enveloped in the recriminations following defeat. Private polls which show the electoral weakness of a party are more depressing for morale than public polls; the party strategists have to sit through a formal presentation of the former. Most politicians appear to regard polls as background information, something to read like a newspaper article; they have their own theories about electoral behaviour, which may relate to the weather, the feeling of prosperity, ideology, time for a change, and so on. And in both parties one still encounters some suspicion about the whole business of sampling and professional communications, as well as politicians who prefer to trust their own judgement of what voters want.

Yet sustained exposure to the private-poll presentations has contributed to an improved understanding of electoral behaviour among politicians and officials – which was an aim of some of the advocates of private polls twenty years ago. The pollster, with the perspective of an outsider, may remind the committed partisan of how remote many of his concerns are to the ordinary voter. Strategists may now use evidence where they once relied on hearsay and other impressions. Reports from the grass roots are also more likely to be considered with a more discerning, even sceptical, eye.[7]

There are several reasons why private polls sometimes fail to be absorbed into the machinery. Campaigns certainly have their elements which are planned and co-ordinated; yet from the inside they can also appear messy, rushed, spontaneous, with many actions resulting from accidents and failures of communication. One suspects that a lot of polling material simply gets 'lost' in the overload of information. (One might add that all this is true of much policy-oriented research.) The other problems are general to all surveys. Polls may show that voters want inconsistent policies, or policies which a party finds politically 'impossible' (for example, for a Labour government to impose legal constraints on trade union pickets). Or the data may be compatible with quite different interpretations and programmes of action. If a party's favoured issue is of low salience, one may as readily interpret this as a basis for emphasising as for ignoring it, and so on. As one frustrated politician commented: 'The polls may give us information about problems but they do not tell us how to solve them.'

The regular use of private opinion polls by parties contrasts with the position twenty years ago. But the scale of polling has not developed since the mid-1960s, and is still modest when compared with the equivalent budgets of political organisations in the USA and West Germany and for testing and marketing the products of commercial companies. Polling has not transformed the nature of election campaigns; parties and the routines of elections appear to have absorbed them, like they have so many other innovations.

Notes: Chapter 13

Dennis Kavanagh was a lecturer in government at the University of Manchester and is now Professor of Government at the University of Nottingham.

1 For a comparative treatment of the role of opinion polls in elections in Western states, see my 'Opinion polls', in David Butler, Howard Penniman and Austin Ranney (eds), *Democracy at the Polls* (Washington, DC: American Enterprise Institute, 1980).
2 See Harold Wilson, 'Market research in the private and public sectors', *Journal of the Market Research Society*, vol. 20, no. 3, 1979.
3 David Butler and Anthony King, *The British General Election of 1964* (London: Macmillan, 1965), p. 69.
4 Apart from being subject to different demands from individual members of the NEC, the Labour pollster also deals directly with the General Secretary, the party leader, the Information Sub-Committee of the NEC, the Organisation Sub-Committee of the NEC, various Transport House officials and the staff of Number 10, Downing Street.
5 Rasmussen interview with Robert Worcester, *British Politics Group Newsletter* (1977), p. 10.
6 MORI made remarkably accurate private predictions for Mr Wilson in both February and October 1974. These predictions were made, however, on the basis of very small samples and were not the main object of the polling operation. It was also very close to the final result in 1979. In 1970 ORC made its reputation by being the only poll to forecast a Conservative lead in the votes. It did this by allowing for differential abstention and projecting from a finding that twenty-two of 275 respondents, interviewed on the day before election day, were changing their voting intentions.
7 With the decline in local party membership and activity, spokesmen for the grass roots may be more isolated from the electorate as a whole. In 1966 the sharp contrast in the reports of the public mood from ORC and Conservative local and regional organisers produced reactions ranging from embarrassment to amusement in Central Office.

14

Labour-Voting conservatives: Policy Differences between the Labour Party and Labour Voters

MARTIN HARROP

There is a sense in which the Labour Party did *not* lose the May 1979 general election. In terms of the electorate's basic partisan allegiances, Labour retained a one-point lead in a survey conducted by Gallup for the BBC on 2–3 May. A separate, post-election survey by the British Election Study at Essex University painted a similar picture. Although this study gave the Tories a two-point lead in party identification, this lead was smaller than its margin in the distribution of the vote among the same sample. If all those electors who thought of themselves as Labour had actually voted Labour on 3 May, the Labour Party might well have won the election and would probably have been able to deny the Tories a working majority in Parliament.

This underperformance by the Labour Party is nothing new in British elections; it has been observed throughout the 1970s in the series of academic surveys begun by Butler and Stokes at Nuffield College, Oxford.[1] The Labour Party should simply be achieving a greater share of the electoral market than it normally does achieve. This failing should be a matter of concern to those Labour Party communicators charged with translating diffuse expressions of support into the hard currency of votes.

Paradoxically, the very ubiquity of this discrepancy between Labour's basic support and its electoral performance reduces the usefulness of the discrepancy as an explanation of Labour's defeat in the specific case of 1979. If the Labour Party receives a smaller share of the vote than of party identification even when it wins elections, the discrepancy observed in 1979 can hardly be regarded as a sufficient explanation of Labour's defeat. Better, perhaps, to concentrate on more specific features of the 1979 campaign. There is some evidence, for example, that the Conservative Party's PEBs on television played an important facilitating role in bringing about this desertion to the

Tories by Labour identifiers in the 1979 campaign. The BBC/Gallup election survey showed that 66 per cent (19 out of 29) Labour-identifying Conservative voters in their sample did not decide which party they were going to vote for until the campaign was under way. The comparable figure for Labour-identifying Labour voters was only 20 per cent. It seems, then, that there must have been *something* in the campaign which accounts for this defection by Labour identifiers. A hint as to what this something might be comes from another question in the BBC survey, a question asking respondents to select from a list of reasons those which were important to their electoral choice. This list included party broadcasts on television: 24 per cent (7 out of 29) Labour-identifying Tory voters cited the Conservatives' broadcasts as a factor in their choice, whereas only 12 per cent of Labour loyalists cited the Labour broadcasts as a reason in their choice. More interestingly, none at all of the dozen Tory-identifying Labour voters in the sample said they had been influenced by Labour's broadcasts. Though the numbers here are much too small to be conclusive, it does seem as though the critical attitude which Tim Bell expresses elsewhere (in Chapter 2) to the campaign PEBs he produced for the Conservative Party is not justified by what evidence is available on their electoral impact.

The purpose of this paper, though, is to examine the broader question of Labour's electoral underperformance. I want to examine one particular explanation for this underperformance, an explanation which focuses on the support offered by many traditional Labour voters to conservative – and often Conservative – policies. Many observers have pointed to what can be regarded in broad, summary terms as the 'right-wing' policy preferences of Labour voters in many areas of economic and social policy, areas which include immigration, capital punishment, law and order, the trade unions and nationalisation. Indeed, each generation of psephologists rediscovers for itself the phenomenon of Labour-voting conservatism and, hence, is in danger of misinterpreting its nature. Surveys conducted in 1950, 1951, 1955, 1959, 1964–74, 1977 and 1979 have pointed to the greater support offered by Tory voters to Conservative principles than is offered by Labour voters to socialist principles.[2] During and after the 1979 election campaign, to take a recent but typical example, Anthony King wrote in the *Observer* of the growing doubts held by many Labour voters about the wisdom of following traditional socialist policies and suggested that such doubts were the main factor accounting for the Tory lead in the polls.

Implicit (though rarely more than that) in many of these surveys is what we might call a 'big bang' image of Labour Party development. Beginning as a small group of people sharing both a critique of capitalism and a vision of a socialist alternative, this image presents the various elements of the party as moving further and further apart as the party grows and develops into a more complex and differentiated organisation. From this perspective, divisions between leaders, activists and voters are seen as a relatively new and, hence, dangerous development. Yet given the findings of the surveys we have cited, and the evidence of more general studies of Labour Party history, one wonders whether a 'steady-state' image of divisions within the Labour Party might not be more appropriate. From this perspective, Labour-voting conservatism would be viewed not so much as a new and potentially de-stabilising phenomenon but would be seen rather as a reflection of normal and continuing features of working-class life in an industrial society. Parkin's notion of the dominant value system or, less fashionably, Lipset's concept of working-class authoritarianism might be invoked to perform the theoretical work here.[3] For Labour Party communicators, this steady-state image has the reassuring implication that policy differences between the party and its voters do not constitute a new and, hence, possibly dangerous threat to the party's electoral strength. If the 'problem' is no worse now than in 1945, 1964, or 1974, can there really be a problem at all?

An informed choice between these two images clearly requires trend data on the policy preferences of Labour voters. Such data is provided in the first part of this paper. The second part examines the social base of Labour-voting conservatism in an attempt to identify the kinds of Labour voters most at risk from conservative appeals. The third part considers whether Labour voters themselves believe there is any discrepancy between their own policy preferences and those of their party. The conclusion speculates on the electoral effects of Labour-voting conservatism and considers its implications for political communication. The answers to all these questions will not provide a direct explanation of Labour's defeat in 1979. Their importance derives rather from the light they cast on a phenomenon which has confronted and often puzzled communicators in both main parties at most postwar elections – and will no doubt continue to do so in 1983–4.

Trends

To identify trends in the policy preferences of Labour voters, I asked Market Opinion Research International to include in a survey they conducted in June 1980 a set of policy questions first asked by Gallup in September 1957 and repeated by Gallup in identical form in

January 1962.[4] In addition, I included a number of extra items – on the unions, immigration, capital punishment and tax cuts – which reflect issues that have emerged since the original surveys were conducted. The results of all three surveys are shown by voting intention in Table 14.1.

The table confirms that Labour-voting conservatism is alive and well in the 1980s. A majority of Labour voters support such conservative policies as reducing black immigration, the return of the death penalty, reducing the power of the unions through legal changes and cutting taxes even at the price of reduced government spending. At the same time, a narrow majority of Labour voters now oppose such traditional socialist policies as cutting defence spending,

Table 14.1 *Proportion of Conservative and Labour Voters Supporting Various Policies, 1957–80*

	Labour			Conservative		
	1957 (%)	1962 (%)	1980 (%)	1957 (%)	1962 (%)	1980 (%)
Introduce price controls on essentials like food and clothing	87	92	91	48	76	79
Restrict dividends and profits	83	89	63	30	59	29
Cut down on defence expenditure	76	75	49	38	54	20
Abolish the House of Lords	61	–	48	19	–	16
Extend nationalisation to more industries	62	68	44	5	7	8
Give more aid to backward countries	50	52	40	51	46	36
Reduce expenditure on the Welfare State	22	34	27	63	52	38
Reduce the number of black immigrants coming into Britain	–	–	80	–	–	88
Cut taxes, even if this means reducing government spending	–	–	70	–	–	67
Bring back the death penalty	–	–	66	–	–	76
Reduce the power of the trade unions by changes in the law	–	–	57	–	–	93

Note:
Base excludes 'don't knows'.
Source:
Gallup, 1957, 1962; MORI, 1980.

abolishing the House of Lords, extending nationalisation and giving more aid to 'backward' countries. The only crumb of comfort for the Labour Party here is that its voters do seem to be willing to support those radical policies, such as price controls and profit restrictions, from which they might expect to gain at least a short-term economic benefit.

A more significant feature of Table 14.1 is its confirmation of a substantial shift to the right among Labour voters since 1962. At that time a majority of Labour voters supported a reduction in defence spending, an extension of nationalisation and increased aid to 'backward' countries. In 1957 too a majority favoured abolition of the House of Lords. Yet by 1980 each of these policies was opposed by at least a small majority of Labour voters. Support for restrictions on dividends and profits also declined substantially between 1962–80, though this particular policy remains popular with a clear majority of Labour voters. The new issues of immigration, union power and the reintroduction of capital punishment also elicit a conservative response from most Labour voters. It is only on the issues of price controls and the maintenance of public expenditure on the welfare state that Labour voters have retained their commitment to a left-wing policy. But note here that there is no simple linear trend to be observed across all three surveys. If anything, Labour voters seem to have moved slightly to the left in the initial period of 1957–62. In such circumstances, a simple extrapolation into the future of the rightward shift observed during 1962–80 would be extremely injudicious. Events will have their say.

A comparison of the figures for supporters of the two main parties shows a substantial decline in polarisation between Conservative and Labour voters since 1957 and, to a much lesser extent, since 1962. In 1957 the mean difference between the proportion of Conservative and Labour voters supporting the policies shown in the table was 39 per cent. By 1980 this had declined to 23 per cent for the same policies. The only issue failing to register a decline in polarisation was overseas aid; and here there was no significant difference between Conservative and Labour voters in the first place. Note that this process of convergence is not just a reflection of the rightward march of the Labour voter; it also reflects a substantial move to the left by Conservative voters on the issues of price controls and the maintenance of expenditure on the welfare state.

The net result of these changes is that Labour voters are now a more divided group than Conservative voters. On eight of the eleven issues in Table 14.1 two Conservative voters selected at random would now be more likely to agree with each other than would two Labour voters to agree with each other. The exceptions are price controls on essentials, the maintenance of welfare state spending and the desirability of cutting taxes even at the price of reduced government expenditure.

The 'steady-state' image of Labour-voting conservatism is clearly inappropriate to these data. There has been a long-term decline in the proportion of Labour voters willing to endorse radical policies, a decline which at least renders more credible the claim that the conservative attitudes of Labour voters may already have been or may in the future prove to be electorally damaging to the Labour Party.

Base

Two main types of Labour-voting conservative can be identified from the MORI survey. The first, more sharply defined category consists of older Labour voters, with limited education, who live in a council house and work if at all in a manual and especially semi- or unskilled occupation. The chief quarrel which this type of voter has with the Labour Party concerns its perceived liberalism on social issues. Such voters adopt a self-consciously tough-minded view of politics, as firm in their opposition to overseas aid and black immigration as they are in their support of capital punishment. On more traditional economic issues, however, voters in this category are quite willing to support radical policies from which one assumes they would expect to benefit.

The second and more shadowy figure lurking in our data is a very different character. Far from adopting a conservative attitude on social issues, people in this category vote Labour precisely because of their liberal attitudes on such issues as immigration and capital punishment. The conservatism of this type is seen on economic issues – in comparatively high levels of opposition to further nationalisation, price controls and restrictions on dividends and profits. Though the social location of people in this category is not so easily identified, one clearly has to move up the social scale – to car and home-owners, certainly, and perhaps into the ranks of the middle class.

The validity of this distinction between different types of Labour-voting conservative is suggested by Table 14.2. This shows which categories of Labour voters are particularly attached to conservative views on the items which, according to a factor analysis not reported here, best represent the social issue (immigration, capital punishment and overseas aid) and the economic issue (dividends and profits, price controls and nationalisation). The profile of Labour's 'dissonants' clearly differs between these two issues. On all three items representing the social issue, working-class and poorly educated Labour voters are significantly more likely than their middle-class, well-educated

Table 14.2 *Groups of Labour Voters Particularly Likely to Support 'conservative' Policies*

Social Issues
'Reduce the number of black immigrants coming into Britain'
  working class
  lives in rented accommodation
  terminal education age 16 or less
  widowed/divorced/separated
'Bring back the death penalty'
  working class
  lives in rented accommodation
  terminal education age 16 or less
  widowed/divorced/separated
  women
'Do not give more aid to backward countries'
  working class
  married
  terminal education age 16 or less
  not a union member

Economic Issues
'Do not restrict dividends and profits'
  car-owners
  single
'Do not introduce price controls on essentials like food and clothing'
  middle class
  head-of-household
'Do not extend nationalisation to more industries'
  car-owners
  home-owners
  full-time workers

Note:
Labour voters with the specified attribute are significantly more likely (at the 0·05 level) to agree with the policy than those without. In the table, the direction of some statements has been reversed from the survey wording to simplify presentation. Age and telephone in home were not significant on any of the six issues.

counterparts to express conservative sentiments. On immigration and capital punishment, Labour-voting conservatives are also more likely than other Labour voters to live in rented, primarily council accommodation and (perhaps reflecting an age effect?) to be widowed, divorced, or separated. In any event, Table 14.2 does demonstrate a clearly defined 'down-market' profile for Labour voters with conservative views on the social issue.

Labour voters with conservative preferences on the economic issue are a more 'up-market' group. Car-owners among the Labour electorate are less likely to support further nationalisation and restrictions on dividends and profits than Labour voters without access to a car. Middle-class Labour voters in general are less likely to support the imposition of price controls than their working-class counterparts. Though the profile is not as sharp as on the social issue, it does seem as though the more affluent a Labour voter is, the less likely is he to support an extension of government involvement in the running of the economy. If education is the principal base of division between Labour voters on the social issue, economic position is – not surprisingly – the principal base of division on the economic issue.

Perceptions

The first question to be asked here is whether voters do in fact associate the Labour Party with the less popular policies in our survey. Such an association is presumably a necessary if not a sufficient condition of electoral damage to Labour resulting from the conservative attitudes of its traditional supporters. I asked respondents whether they thought the Conservative Party, the Labour Party, or both, supported these policies. The results, shown in Table 14·3, offer little reassurance to the Labour Party. Of the five most widely supported policies, four are more likely to be associated with the Tories than with Labour, the exception being the most popular policy of all – price controls on essentials. Of the five least popular policies, on the other hand, four are more likely to be associated with Labour than with the Conservatives. In this case, the exception is the issue of reducing expenditure on the welfare state. It is clear that the Labour Party in 1980 is simply very badly positioned in the policy market-place.

But do Labour voters themselves believe there is a discrepancy between their own views and those of their party? It might be argued, after all, that one of the few compensations of being a divided party is that supporters can see in the party whatever they wish to see, hence limiting the electoral damage inflicted by a policy profile which is unpopular with the electorate as a whole. In fact however there are, as Table 14.4 shows, clear limits to the power of selective perception. This table shows what proportion of Labour voters believe the Conservatives but not Labour support their views on a given policy. On the issue of nationalisation, for example, the table shows that 45 per cent of all Labour voters oppose further nationalisation and believe that the Conservatives but not Labour oppose further

Table 14.3 *Perceptions of Party Policy*

	Proportion believing the policy is supported by	
	Labour (%)	Conservative (%)
Introduce price controls on essentials like food and clothing (86%)	66	15
Reduce the number of black immigrants coming into Britain (84%)	21	62
Reduce the power of the trade unions by changes in the law (75%)	6	83
Bring back the death penalty (71%)	16	36
Cut taxes, even if this means reducing government spending (69%)	28	49
Restrict dividends and profits (47%)	64	16
Give more aid to backward countries (38%)	43	29
Cut down on defence expenditure (35%)	59	18
Abolish the House of Lords (33%)	65	5
Reduce expenditure on the welfare state (32%)	10	70
Extend nationalisation to more industries (25%)	75	9

Note:
Figure in brackets shows percentage of electorate in favour.
Source:
MORI.

nationalisation.[5] For purposes of comparison, the table also shows the proportion of Conservative voters believing that Labour rather than the Conservatives support their own views on the policy in question. The main conclusion to be drawn here is that Labour-voting conservatives substantially outnumber Tory-voting socialists. Taking the average of all eleven issues in the table, 29 per cent of Labour voters prefer the policy of the Conservative Party to that of the Labour Party.[6] The equivalent figure for Conservative voters preferring Labour policy is a smaller but still perhaps surprisingly large 21 per cent. There are only three issues where more Conservative voters prefer Labour policy than Labour voters prefer Conservative policy: price controls, expenditure on the welfare state and the issue of tax cuts vs government spending. Note too that Labour only escapes relatively lightly on the issue of capital punishment because just 27 per cent of pro-capital punishment Labour voters believe the Conservative

Table 14.4 *Voters' Perceptions of Differences between Their Own Views and Those of the Major Parties*

	Proportion of Labour voters who believe the Conservatives but not Labour support their views on the issue (%)	Proportion of Conservative voters who believe Labour but not the Conservatives support their views on the issue (%)
Nationalisation	45	6
Use of the law to reduce trade union power	45	7
Black immigration	40	13
House of Lords	31	11
Dividend and profit restrictions	30	23
Aid to backward countries	29	28
Defence expenditure	27	18
Cut taxes, or maintain government spending	24	28
Expenditure on the welfare state	19	45
Death penalty	17	9
Price controls on essentials	12	44

Source:
MORI.

Party supports the re-introduction of the death penalty. Labour voters who support capital punishment but believe that neither main party agrees with them may still be at risk to the minor parties or abstention, even if they have little incentive to transfer to the Conservative Party on this issue.

Conclusion

The key question is: how many votes has Labour lost, or might it lose in the future, as a result of this phenomenon of Labour-voting conservatism? Key question though this may be, it is also extremely difficult to answer in any satisfactory way. A precise estimate of the effect of a particular policy on voting behaviour calls for repeated interviews with the same people and long-term panel data of this kind are not currently available for the 1974–9 period. But the tenor of much survey research suggests the limited impact of policy preferences on electoral choice in general and on the voting behaviour of Labour voters in particular.[7] While some of the issues we have considered might exert a large negative impact on Labour's strength under particular political circumstances, it seems likely that these effects will continue to be overwhelmed by the success or failure of the party at presenting itself as the party of the working class and as the party most capable of running the economy successfully. At least in calm waters, therefore, one would normally expect a well-led Labour Party to avoid foundering on the by now well-charted rocks of Labour-voting conservatism. But if the new skipper should choose to disregard the charts altogether, the officers might be well advised to at least consider the advantages of mutiny.

But the modest impact (if such it is) of Labour-voting conservatism on the relative strength of Britain's two major parties may partly reflect failures of party strategy. For there is a sense in which our findings suggest a complete reversal in the tone currently adopted by the Conservative and Labour parties in their political communication. One of the continuing paradoxes of British politics is that the Labour Party is more concerned with policy than with image, yet benefits from its image rather than its policies, while the Conservative Party has in recent elections seemed at least as concerned with image as with policy, yet benefits from its policies rather than its image. Electorally speaking, the strength of the Labour Party lies in what it is rather than what it does; whereas the reverse is true of the Conservative Party. Both parties, one feels, would do well to re-orient their communications around their strengths rather than weaknesses, though it is doubtless harder for a Conservative Party confronting the problems of government to emphasise its effectiveness than it should be for a Labour Party in opposition to emphasise its concern for the well-being of ordinary people. In particular, one suspects that the Conservative Party could, if it wished, exploit the social issue more vigorously and to greater electoral effect than it has done hitherto. Over the postwar period, the traditionalists in the Tory Party have lost ground to the Tory pragmatists, who claim that the quickest route to the working-class vote now lies through an appeal to their economic interests rather than their deferential attitudes. Should these same pragmatists be willing to swallow their inhibitions and begin to play the emerging social issue with the same skill they have applied to the economic issue, the position of the Labour Party, with its deep and probably immutable divisions between a well-educated liberal leadership and a poorly educated conservative base, might prove unenviable indeed.[8]

Notes: Chapter 14

Martin Harrop is a lecturer in politics at the University of Newcastle upon Tyne.

1 Since these surveys usually compare party identification with voting *intentions*, simple abstention cannot be the explanation. The proportion actually voting Labour will normally be lower again than the proportion saying they intend to do so.
2 M. Benney, A. P. Gray and R. H. Pear, *How People Vote* (London: Routledge & Kegan Paul, 1956), pp. 139–54, pp. 190–202; R. S. Milne and H. C. Mackenzie, *Straight Fight* (London: Hansard Society, 1954), pp. 100–12 and *Marginal Seat 1955* (London: Hansard Society, 1958), pp. 108–27; M. Abrams and R. Rose, *Must Labour Lose?* (Harmondsworth: Penguin, 1960), p. 36; I. Crewe, B. Sarlvik and J. Alt, 'Partisan dealignment in Britain, 1964–1974', *British Journal of Political Science*, vol. VII, no. 4 (1977), p. 152.
3 F. Parkin, *Class Inequality and Political Order* (New York: Praeger, 1971); S. Lipset, 'Democracy and working-class authoritarianism', *American Sociological Review*, vol. XXIV, no. 4 (1959), pp. 482–501.
4 The MORI sample was a nationally representative quota sample of 961 respondents interviewed in 158 sampling points. The questions analysed herein came near the beginning of a multi-purpose survey with a modal interview length of 26–35 minutes. To maintain comparability with the earlier surveys, the odd introductory wording 'Do you think the party which gets your vote should support or oppose these proposals?' was retained. My thanks to the Nuffield Foundation for their financial support of this research.
5 The 45 per cent also includes a few idiosyncratic respondents who support more nationalisation but believe that the Tories rather than Labour support more nationalisation.
6 Actually, it is misleading to speak of 'preferences' here, since some voters who agree with the policy of just one party on an issue may still for some reason express a preference for the policy of another party on that same issue. But such respondents were a small group in February 1974 and are probably still so in 1980. See J. E. Alt, B. Sarlvik and I. Crewe, 'Partisanship and political choice: issue preferences in the British electorate', *British Journal of Political Science*, vol. VI, no. 3 (1976), pp. 273–91.
7 For evidence that Labour voters are less likely than Conservatives to see the political world in policy terms, see J. Alt, B. Sarlvik and I. Crewe, 'Individual differences scaling and group attitude structures: British party imagery in 1974', *Quality and Quantity*, vol. X, no. 4 (1976), p. 310; *NOP Political Bulletin* (June–July 1970) p. 4, and Market & Opinion Research International, *British Public Opinion: General Election 1979, Final Report* (London: MORI, 1979), p. 52.
8 MORI conducted a more recent survey of the electorate's policy preferences for the *Sunday Times* in July 1980, a survey which nicely complements the one reported here.

The Polls: Discussion

Crewe/McKee

Peter Madgwick (University College of Wales)
I wonder whether Ivor was implying that the media were doing a disservice to democracy by keeping people interested in the election?

Ivor Crewe
That is two questions, isn't it? First, do polls help the media to maintain the electorate's interest in the election? Secondly, is this a good or bad thing? The answer to the first question is 'yes, I think so'. Possibly excepting the last day or two of the campaign, the function of polls for the media is not really to supply the media with accurate information about the state of the electorate, though I think they *do* provide more accurate information than anything else. Rather, the function of polls for the media is to provide a ready-made pre-scheduled story, which doesn't involve a lot of fact gathering by journalists since all the facts are gathered by the poll company. Polls will always be news; I don't think there is such a thing as an unnewsworthy poll. Now, whether this is a good thing or a bad thing is a matter of personal political predilections. I think it is a good thing on the whole, though I don't see why my view should be more important than anybody else's.

Richard Rose
To Paul McKee: how would you feel about doing polls to be presented within forty-five minutes of the real result if you got the kind of poll that the BBC got in October 1974? Within the course of forty-five minutes or an hour, the 'exclusive' story has to be quietened down because it's too exclusive and not very credible either.

Paul McKee
In October 1974 the BBC came up with a prediction of a Labour landslide for three-quarters of an hour and then it was like the mighty steam-engine suddenly realising and going into reverse. It was a classic case there of the dangers of doing a national poll and converting it straightforwardly into a seat prediction. If you are doing a seat prediction, it is not enough to simply take a national poll. I believe quite strongly that if you are going to do a seat prediction you have to concentrate on the Con/Lab marginals first of all, but equally important, you have to concentrate on the other types of seats which might change hands – for example, the SNP/Con contests, the SNP/Lab, Con/Lib and the Lab/Lib contests. You have to have separate samples in each of these types if you are in the business of making a seat projection. Now, the reason why not many people are in the business of making seat projections is because it is jolly expensive. A brief comment while I'm speaking on what Ivor Crewe was saying about why the media use polls in an election campaign. Ivor was implying that polls are a quick, easy and by implication a cheap way of filling space. In fact, polls are really the most expensive way that newspapers

have of filling space; they don't do it simply for that reason. Motives are mixed but in a large number of cases, polls are commissioned as an information exercise, as a deliberate way of informing people. They may perform this function badly, there are some terrible examples of bad reporting of polls, but in a significant number of cases polls are taken as a way of informing the public about the state of the 'horse race' within the constraints of space and time which are available to report the results.

Peter Kellner

I would just like to say that I have the good fortune to represent a paper that wasn't published during the election and which, therefore, avoided all these problems. My question relates specifically to 'quickie' polls, with a supplementary to Paul McKee. I remember one or two rogue polls in the February 1974 campaign. Lou Harris had one showing a Tory lead much larger than everyone else's. My impression was that this might have been due to fairly straightforward design errors, such as the use of non-interlocking quotas. It must be possible to get empirical evidence on the characteristics of respondents in 'quickie' samples. Does the sample have a correct proportion of trade union members, council-house tenants, owner-occupiers, telephone owners? There is no particular reason why with a decent interlocking sample they should be more inaccurate than a random sample, and if they are, it's something that should be investigated. So my question is: what evidence is there on this point? The subsidiary to Paul is this. I take all your points about leaving people to go to the newspapers for full information on polls. But the one thing which ITN did leave out was fieldwork dates. When you are presenting polls, you convey the impression you are reporting public opinion now. I would have thought it is important to give fieldwork dates of each poll even in secondary stories.

Ivor Crewe

That's a good question; I wish I had the answers. I don't. I too would like to know what differences there are in the backgrounds of people interviewed in one-day polls as opposed to two- or three-day polls. I would like more information about 'quickie' polls. Is the poll done during daylight hours alone or is it also done in the evening? This presumably makes some difference to the number of employed people one will interview at least if employment status is not part of the quota itself.

Paul McKee

A brief comment on 'quickie' polls. I think the empirical evidence indicates that it is easier for interviewers to fudge their quotas when they have a long time to fill it rather than a short time. So I don't personally take the same view as Ivor Crewe does about the dangers in 'quickie' polls; there are some dangers in polls spread over a long period of time. So on to the point directed to me about fieldwork dates. Peter Kellner has a very valid point. We reported fieldwork dates in one or two of the earlier polls we covered, but as the campaign proceeded, we found the polls did relate to the day of, or the day before, the broadcast. We phased fieldwork dates out to save time though in the last seven days, and in particular on the closing polls, we did try to indicate fieldwork dates so as to report the trend.

Barter

Ivor Crewe
The national polls had a very good record but the polls of individual constituencies did not. I'm thinking not only of the Marplan polls in three Midlands constituencies for the *Birmingham Mail*, but also the Abacus polls of four Welsh constituencies which in some cases were way out, amazingly out. The question I want to ask John Barter is: why is it more difficult for polls to get single constituency results right?

John Barter
I'm not sure that your premises is totally justified. The record of the major polling organisations in by-elections is reasonably good when they have gone on polling until very close to the election. The lesson all of us have learned over the years is that it's really more important to go on asking the questions to the very last minute than it is to worry about the fine points of sampling – though by all means worry about sampling if you can. Now, that's actually quite difficult to do in a by-election. The reason is that it's difficult to get the number of interviewers into a by-election which would enable you to get a good sample size at the last possible moment. It's an expensive thing to do, actually. It's considerably more expensive to do a by-election properly than to do a national election poll, because you've got to shift interviewers into the place.

Ivor Crewe
Granted it's more expensive, none the less once it's been done, one would still like to know why the results are so out.

Denis Balsom (University College of Wales)
I know a little bit about the Welsh polls. I was involved with the Abacus ones for BBC Wales. There were, I think, a number of technical problems. There was also another series of five constituency polls in Wales for the *Western Mail* in which Research and Marketing Ltd were involved. They also had some errors. I think inexperience was a major factor in both cases.

Gordon Heald
I don't think there's any simple explanation. I also think that the track-record hasn't been very good; we've got slightly tarnished in by-election polls. I instinctively feel that it's due to excessive clustering. I think the golden rule about polls is to get as wide a geographical spread as possible. The trouble with small constituency polls is that you've got twenty interviewers in there doing fifteen interviews each. I don't know why, I just feel instinctively that you've got errors coming through excessive clustering.

Paul Whiteley
I was interested to hear John Barter say that NOP has now gone over

completely to quota sampling with its election polls. Could he say a bit more about the interlocking quotas he uses? For the purist statistician all the statistics for calculating error margins don't apply with quota samples. I don't take that purist line myself but some do. What's your view?

John Barter
Can I just say something in parentheses on that? One of the things Ivor Crewe raised in his paper was that we didn't say enough about what the error margin is in polls. I'm not so sure that we should say more about this. In fact, on the polls that we're using, we don't know what the error is. It may well be *less* than it is on a random sample. Nobody can prove it either way. Our sample design is broadly as follows. First of all, we take a sample of constituencies. The voting record of these constituencies matches the overall voting figures at the last election. (I think I'm speaking for all the pollsters there.) We then set interlocking age, sex and class quotas from the information we have available for these selected constituencies. By interlocking we make sure that we don't end up with, for example, an excess of older men simply because they're retired and living at home. We set an additional working/not-working quota for women. Then finally what we do – and what Bob Worcester also does – is to have something which we don't set as a quota but which we look at afterwards, something like trade union membership. If we find we're wildly out on trade union membership, then we would weight the results for that particular variable.

James Rothman
Could I make one technical point? I can't let John Barter get away with saying that you can't measure the sampling error of quota samples. That's just not true.

Ian Budge (University of Essex)
The question which occurred to me after the presentations was the question of turnout. In your tables and discussion, you obviously tried as far as possible to ignore the question of turnout.

John Barter
In fact, I think most of the polls have at various times tried adjusting for turnout by measuring reported certainty of voting. On the whole, this doesn't seem to work very well and so the best thing you can do, I think, is ignore it. Other people may disagree.

Bob Worcester
We don't ignore it in terms of question wording. What we're doing in the end is ignoring it in terms of 'forecast'. Certainly, the 1970 ORC victory in forecasting a Conservative victory was based on a turnout weighting (as well as a late shift in voting intentions) that took them over the line from a Labour to a Conservative victory. Now, the point is they explained how they did it. My view is that any jiggery-pokery like that should be explained – and sometimes it isn't. One thing that I thought was fascinating in the *Sunday Times* panel

study was that the panel effect of repeated interviews didn't seem to affect voting intentions, but it increased turnout to 92 per cent.

Kavanagh

Jack Brand
The crucial question is whether the parties get value for money as far as the polls are concerned, and it seems to me that the answer is different depending on the kind of party you are. If you are a party which essentially wants to get power and is prepared to be very flexible about the sort of things that you do in order to get power, then the information that the pollsters give you is very valuable indeed, because it tells you in the short time within which a certain decision has to be made how to get the most votes. But if on the other hand you are the kind of party that wants to change the way society is run (and this applies to the left wing of the Labour Party and to nationalist parties), then the sort of information that polls give you doesn't really have the same status. If you start taking the pollsters' advice that you should sail along with public opinion, then you are going to depart from your main aim of changing society.

Dennis Kavanagh
It can be said that polls are inherently a conservatising influence in so far as a party that is interested in changing public opinion is perhaps less interested in taking a reading of public opinion and then fitting its own policies into that framework. What it sees is a source of data that it wants to change. That is, I think, a coherent, defensible point of view. The other question is the $64,000 question of whether the parties think they get value for their money. Do you know, by and large, I don't think that is a question that many politicians and party organisers actually ask themselves. Examples of people who run election campaigns actually thinking through what they are doing – and asking whether there are better ways of doing it – are very few and far between. I am much more impressed with the element of ritual in campaigns. It has been my impression that the people who come in from the outside are really quite shocked at the innocence with which party organisers and elected politicians approach the whole business of communication. But I think those who do actually think it through, by and large, don't think they got value for money from the polls. Now, whether their reasoning is valid is another question altogether. One frequent reaction in the Conservative Party is that ORC didn't tell us anything that we didn't already have hunches about. Well, of course it can be very useful to have this kind of evidence to confirm hunches, which are very often wrong. In addition, many politicians don't think polls are useful where polls show a static picture. Again, however, if you hadn't been doing the polls, you wouldn't have spotted any changes which were occurring. In the Labour Party's case, if they feel that they didn't get value out of the polls, this may well be due to the way that the Labour Party organised its campaign. So a lot of politicians think that they did not get value for money from the polls but I would question the validity of the criteria they apply.

John Barter
It seems to me that the distinction which we have just run up between needing polls because you want to conform to public opinion, and not needing polls if you want to convert public opinion, is entirely spurious. You need the information just as much if you want to convert the public, because you want to know what exactly it is people fear and how to allay these anxieties. The second point is an objection to the view that poll information is redundant, because politicians already 'hunch' the right answers. Before you present the findings of any poll, ask the twelve people in the room what they think the findings are going to be and you will get twelve different answers.

Mallory Wober
I feel that what you are calling a private opinion poll ought to be called a public opinion poll. Have you encountered any views from idealists within the parties or from journalists outside the parties to the effect that these things are in some respects public opinion polls of which the findings thereof should not be private?

Ivor Crewe
A comment on the politicians' complaint that the polls aren't very useful because they don't provide information which aids practical decision-making. In one sense this is not an entirely unjustified lament by the politicians. But the parties use the polls for only one part of what they need to know about public opinion in order to act effectively. The immediate readings of public opinion taken by the parties don't provide politicians with what we might call a theory of campaign strategy and that is why the polls are found not to be useful. Let me give an example. It very often happens that a poll will tell a party that it is behind on a really important issue but ahead on a somewhat less important issue. Now, what does a party do in those circumstances? Does it concentrate on the really important issue and try and catch up? Or does it say no, we will concentrate on the less important issue where we are ahead and try and make it more important? It seems to me that the polls certainly in the Labour Party have never given us any real guidance as to how to resolve that kind of dilemma. This is, perhaps, the fault of the parties rather than the pollsters. The parties have not used the polls to provide them with the information that could form the basis of a theory of campaign strategy. At a more detailed level, it also strikes me that the polls are used far too little (certainly by the Labour Party) to test campaign slogans; the polls aren't used for marketing. In that sense, it seems to me that the polls have been used in very limited ways and have provided only a part of the information needed by a party to plan its campaign properly.

Dennis Kavanagh
The Conservatives do use the polls more continuously and they do tend to go in for more marketing of slogans, themes, and so on, than does the Labour Party. The Tories tend to use the polls along the lines Ivor was suggesting the Labour Party should actually do. Mallory Wober asked about the public release of private polls. Yes, there is some pressure. The Labour Party has lodged its private polls in the SSRC Survey archive at Essex University, though

the material can't be used until after the following election. The Conservative Party with a rather enlightened regime over the last couple of years has been receptive to letting Butler and myself use the material, and I think the data will be made available in the long run. An important point which we haven't touched on is the expertise, or rather the lack of it, with which politicians actually read poll data. Some politicians really can't see the significance of data and many more are just downright sceptics.

Appendix 1: Extracts from Conservative Party Political Broadcasts, 1979 General Election

Page 15 (a)

This country was once the finest nation on earth. We were famous for our love of freedom, justice and fair play. Our inventions brought the world out of the Middle Ages to industrial prosperity. 'Made in Britain' meant the best in the world. Our armed forces stood alone against the mightiest army the world had ever seen. Today we are famous for discouraging people from getting to the top. Famous for not rewarding skill, talent and effort. Because it pays people not to work, today less and less is made in Britain. We pay our armed forces less, yet we expect them to do more. Instead of fighting for the country, they're fighting fires or emptying dustbins. In a word, Britain is going backward.

Page 15 (b)

Backwards or forwards – because we can't go on as we are. Not if we're ever going to recreate the prosperity of this nation. We Conservatives want to give people the incentive to work harder. After all, you can't stimulate economies, you can only stimulate people. That way we shall all do well – for ourselves and for Britain. Don't just hope for a better life – vote for one.

Page 18 (a)

Since Labour came to power in 1974, the working man is paying more tax than ever before. More direct taxes, like income tax, and more indirect taxes. In fact, more tax on almost everything you earn and much of what you buy. No other major industrialised country in the world extracts a higher rate of income tax from its citizens than the present Labour government. This government collects a staggering £110,000,000 a day in tax. Now, what is the effect of all this taxation?

> *Wage-earner*: 'If Labour takes so much of our pay packet in taxes, I'll have to ask *him* for more pay.'
>
> *Manufacturer*: 'And if higher taxes make him want more pay, I'll have to cover the costs by putting up my prices to *him*.'
>
> *Shop-keeper*: 'And if he puts his prices up, I've got to pass them on to *her*.'
>
> *Housewife*: 'If he puts his prices up, I'll have to ask my husband for more housekeeping.'
>
> *Wage-earner*: 'And if she wants more housekeeping, I'll have to ask *him* for even more pay.'
>
> *Manufacturer*: 'And if he does that, *I* could go bust – and that won't help the economy or the unemployment problem.'
>
> *Wage-earner*: 'And *I* won't have a job.'

Today, if all the people who didn't have a job went to Westminster to lobby their MP, how far do you think the queue would stretch? Well, it would be a very long way. As far as Birmingham? No, further than that. To Blackburn, perhaps? No, further. To Newcastle? No, further still. It would stretch over 300 miles, to Glasgow.

Page 18 (b)

'Excuse me, is this the queue for the 50p stalls?'
'No, this is the queue for the unemployed.'
'Excuse me, is this the queue for the 50p stalls?'
'Oh no, this is the queue for urgent operations.'
'50p stalls?'
'No. That is the queue for a proper job.'
'Is this the queue for the 50p stalls?'
'No, this is the queue for buying your own council house.'
'Yeah, it's hardly moved in the last four years.'

Nowadays, the country seems to be standing still. Waiting for jobs, operations, homes, everything.

'Is this the queue for the 50p stalls?'
'50p. Haven't you heard of inflation?'

'Tell you what I'd like to see – Labour in power again.'
'Labour in Power – is that the Marx Brothers?'
'No. Another bunch of comedians.'

Coming shortly – the Conservatives. A great programme for all the family.

Page 21

Who cares about Jane? Like a lot of children, Jane is good at some subjects at school; not so good at others. She really could do better if she had some additional attention. Yet when the class is this size, try as they may, teachers just can't cope. Any country that neglects the future of its children neglects its own future. In all these areas, both parties care. Even Labour have plenty of good intentions; but caring that works costs cash.

> *Whitelaw*: 'The trouble with the Labour Party is that they don't learn any lessons from their failures. They certainly care about the unemployed, but the queues grow longer and longer. They're always talking about caring, but talk isn't enough. Real caring must be judged by results. The one certain result of the last four years is that there are now more people in need of care. You will see that our policy is to translate our care into practical results. For our sick, because they need it. For our old, because they've earned it. For our children, because they are our future.'

Page 22 (a)

Labour's policy of low rewards and high taxation has actively discouraged businesses and individuals from increasing production. That's why the average weekly wage of the British worker is so much less than that of French and German workers. In fact it's so low that if the average British worker lived in France or Germany, he wouldn't pay any income tax at all because he would be regarded as a low-paid worker. No wonder we produce less, we're paid less. No wonder we're paid less, we produce less.

Page 22 (b)

Yes, technically this is a party political broadcast on behalf of the Conservative Party. But tonight I don't propose to use the time to make party political points. I don't think you'd want me to do so. The crisis that our country faces is too serious for that. And it is our country, the whole nation, that faces this crisis – not just one party or even one government. This is no time to put party before country. I start from there.

There will be no solution to our difficulties which does not include some restriction on the power of the unions. And if that case is overwhelming, then in the national interest surely government and opposition could make common cause on this one issue. I'm not suggesting that the Labour Party should take over all our Conservative policies on industrial relations. I wouldn't object if they did but it's hardly realistic. If the present crisis has taught us anything, it's surely taught us that we have to think of others as well as ourselves. But no one, however strong his case, is entitled to pursue it by hurting others. There are wreckers among us who don't believe this, but the vast majority of us, and that includes the vast majority of trade unionists, do believe it whether we call ourselves Labour, Conservative, Liberal – or simply British. It's to that majority that I'm talking this evening. We have to learn again to be one nation or one day we shall be no nation.

Page 24 (a)

'Crisis, what crisis? . . .'

It hasn't been a lot of fun living in Britain these last few years, has it? And what a winter. All in all, five years of Labour have left Britain poorer because it penalises those who want to get on. It's left people who do want to work hard and get the best for themselves and their families feeling guilty – and the rest envious if they succeed.

'Did you or did you not want better schooling for your children?'
'Guilty.'
'Now, did you or did you not want to buy your own home?'
'Guilty.'
'Did you or did you not make a profit last year?'
'Guilty.'
'Right. You're sentenced to nationalisation. That should put an end to that.'

'I put it to you that you, a pensioner, expected to pay less tax on your savings just because you've spent forty-five years working for them.'
'Guilty.'

'Is it not true that simply because you've spent three years training for a skilled job, you expected to earn more?'
'Guilty.'

'Is it not a fact that you failed to buy your weekend joint again because you claim it's too expensive?'
'Guilty.'
'But I understand that you and your family had a holiday this year?'

The Labour philosophy taxes ambition –

'Guilty.'
- enthusiasm
'Guilty.'
- achievement
'Guilty.'
- the very things that create wealth, the things that made Britain great.

Page 24 (b)
What do you think should be done to help people pay less tax?

Howe: 'Now obviously the government has to collect money, to pay for our schools, hospitals, police, defence and so on. The question is, how should we raise it? Basically, there's a choice of two ways. You can tax what people earn – then they have to pay, whether they like it or not. As we've seen, too much of that seems to slow down production. Or you can tax some of what people spend. Then at least they have some choice. But, I can almost hear you saying, won't that put up prices? The answer must be not to put tax on essentials, the things we have to buy like food, housing, fuel, public transport, children's clothes and so on, and at the same time to protect pensioners from any price increases.'

On income tax, would you bring income tax down?

Howe: 'That's Conservative policy.'

On Social Services? Do you agree that we should spend the taxpayer's money on the Social Services as our first priority?

Howe: 'That's Conservative policy too.'

On housing, would you give council and new town tenants who want to buy their own homes the right to do so?

Heseltine: 'That's Conservative policy too.'

Now it wouldn't surprise me at all if almost every person in Britain agreed with your decisions. Not because they're Conservative policies but because they're common sense.

Page 25
The Five-Year Tragedy

'Twas the disaster of 'seventy-four
With Wilson, Callaghan and Ross and a few dozen more.
They came to power at the General Election
The world held its breath at the voters' selection.
But there's no going back in a democracy,
Once you've cast your vote, that's how it must be.
On unemployment they got off to a very good start;
Nineteen thousand people decided to part
From the shores of Scotland for evermore,
To go to far lands to see what they had in store.
They must have divined what was to come
They'd looked in the crystal ball and decided to run.
The rest of us stayed here and hoped for the best,
Unaware of the disaster that was to put us to the test.
Then came the winter of 'seventy-eight,
The workers were filled with venom and hate;

Our country was ill, in a very bad state . . .
If the ghosts of our fathers were still alive
At this terrible sight they must surely have died.
Adam Smith, Walter Scott, James Watt too
David Hume, Robbie Burns, to mention a few.
As another poet once did write
'That was our winter of discontent'.
Without a doubt, it was last winter he meant.
But you'll be glad to hear my tale must end,
Before I drive you all quite round the bend
With this story of gloom and great tragedy.
Even the SNP in Parliament were forced to see
That an election was called for. It had to come
And at last through the clouds we could see the sun.
The story is over, we're on the last act.
It'll be a miracle if Jim isn't sacked.
My moral is this: before you start a story
If you want the end to be happy, you'd better vote Tory.

Appendix 2: Political Studies Association Conference, 'Political Communications and the 1979 General Election', University of Newcastle, 14–16 April 1980

List of Participants

Geoffrey Alderman	(Royal Holloway College, University of London)
Linda Anderson	(BBC)
Bonnie Angelo	(*Time* magazine)
Denis Balsom	(University College of Wales)
John Barter	(MD, NOP)
J. M. Beer	(University of Liverpool)
Tim Bell	(MD, Saatchi & Saatchi)
Hugh Berrington	(University of Newcastle)
John Bochel	(University of Dundee)
Jack Brand	(University of Strathclyde)
Ian Budge	(University of Essex)
A. Clark	(Open University)
Ivor Crewe	(University of Essex)
Barry Day	(McCann-Erickson)
Tim Delaney	(Leagas Delaney Advertising)
Graham Dosset	(Gallup)
James Garrett	(James Garrett & Partners)
Ian Gordon	(Kingston Polytechnic)
Brian Gosschalk	(MORI)
Michael Gurevitch	(Open University)
M. Harrison	(University of Keele)
Martin Harrop	(University of Newcastle)
Gordon Heald	(MD, Gallup)
Jenny Jeger	(GJW)
Dennis Kavanagh	(University of Manchester – now Nottingham)
Peter Kellner	(*Sunday Times* – now *New Statesman*)
David Lipsey	(Former adviser, Labour Party; *New Society*)
Paul McKee	(ITN)
P. J. Madgwick	(University College of Wales)
Karl-Peter Markl	(West Germany)
Austin Mitchell	(Labour MP, Grimsby)
John Morrison	(ITN)
Bruce Page	(*New Statesman*)
Malcolm Penwarden	(Gallup)
Michael Pilsworth	(Parliamentary Broadcasting Research Project)
P. G. J. Pulzer	(Christ Church, Oxford)
Adam Raphael	(*Observer*)
Tim Rathbone	(Conservative MP, Lewes)
Richard Rose	(University of Strathclyde)

James Rothman	(Polling adviser, Liberal Party)
Bob Self	(City of London Polytechnic)
Colin Seymour-Ure	(University of Kent)
A. Smith	(University of Kent)
Harvey Thomas	(Conservative Central Office)
Paul Whiteley	(University of Bristol)
Mallory Wober	(IBA)
Bob Worcester	(MD, MORI – Labour private pollster)

Index